Alice Smith's *Beyond the Vei*
While Chapter 1 alone i
the bonus features just k
know how to discern Go.. ...........ions for this critical
hour, this is the place to start.

**GEORGE OTIS, JR.**
*President, The Sentinel Group*
*Lynwood, Washington*

*Beyond the Veil* is full of revelation that will transform your life.
Alice Smith doesn't just *know* about intercession, but lives an
intercessory life before the throne of God. Your prayer group will
greatly benefit from these golden nuggets from the heart of God.

**CINDY JACOBS**
*President, Generals of Intercession*
*Colorado Springs, Colorado*

Intimacy with God is the key to all victorious warfare. Alice Smith's
*Beyond the Veil* is one of God's special tools to help intercessors
understand and apply this vital key. It could revolutionize
your understanding of intimate intercession.

**DICK EASTMAN**
*International President, Every Home for Christ*
*Colorado Springs, Colorado*

Alice is passionately inviting us to go beyond the
veil with the Father. In *Beyond the Veil*, she offers an
invitation we shouldn't ignore.

**CHRIS MITCHELL**
*Christian Broadcasting Network News*
*Virginia Beach, Virginia*

Reading *Beyond the Veil* has sparked within me an even deeper intensity for God. Alice so skillfully weaves the depth of God's call and the deep yearning within intercessors to respond and seek His face. I could not put it down. I believe the holy call for intimacy that is now coming forth is more clearly reached here than in anything else I've read. I was taken beyond the veil and desired to dwell there.

**BOBBYE BYERLY**
*U.S. National President, AGLOW International*
*Lynwood, Washington*

God has gifted Alice Smith with much-needed insights into the ministry of intercession which arise from her unique combination of deep spiritual sensitivity, solid biblical foundation and a consistent record of ministry to the entire body of Christ. This book is the result. Read it! It is an absolute must for the intercessory ministry that must envelop a city-reaching thrust.

**ED SILVOSO**
*Founder, Harvest Evangelism*
*San Jose, California*

Rarely are books so challenging and yet so reassuring. Alice Smith dispels the phony elitism and guilt that can surround the word *intercessor*. Somehow, even as she encourages those specially called as intercessors, she manages to welcome everyone to the practice of intercession.

**STEVE HAWTHORNE**
*WayMakers*
*Austin, Texas*

*Beyond the Veil* is one of the final pieces of the puzzle to mobilizing intercessors to partner with God in prayer. This book is like a dressing room to equip the saints. Alice Smith takes you, the intercessor, from the outer court into the holy of holies. It is filled with valuable, personal insights from one of God's chief prayer warriors that will enable any intercessor to go beyond the veil.

**STEVE SHANKLIN**
*National Prayer Manager, Promise Keepers*
*Denver, Colorado*

*Beyond the Veil* is a call to intercession for the purpose of advancing God's kingdom and undergirding evangelism. Alice Smith shows how effective intercession involves intimacy with Christ through His Spirit, joining with Him in what He is doing (John 5:15; Romans 8:26,34). In this book, she effectively employs typological interpretation of the Tabernacle to offer us a picture of what it means to enter the Lord's presence through intimate intercession.

**GARY S. GREIG**
*Associate Professor of the Old Testament*
*Regent University, School of Divinity*
*Virginia Beach, Virginia*

Alice Smith meets us where we are. *Beyond the Veil* communicates intercession from a practical level, where learning is a pleasure and passion for more of Him becomes a treasure. For what Alice has received from countless hours at His feet, she desires to impart. Read, relish and intercede!

**JILL GRIFFITH**
*Jill Griffith Ministries*
*Colorado Springs, Colorado*

# Beyond the Veil

Alice Smith

**Regal**

From Gospel Light
Ventura, California, U.S.A.

PUBLISHED BY REGAL BOOKS
FROM GOSPEL LIGHT
VENTURA, CALIFORNIA, U.S.A.

**Regal** PRINTED IN THE U.S.A.

Regal Books is a ministry of Gospel Light, a Christian publisher dedicated to serving the local church. We believe God's vision for Gospel Light is to provide church leaders with biblical, user-friendly materials that will help them evangelize, disciple and minister to children, youth and families.

It is our prayer that this Regal book will help you discover biblical truth for your own life and help you meet the needs of others. May God richly bless you.

*For a free catalog of resources from Regal Books/Gospel Light, please call your Christian supplier or contact us at* 1-800-4-GOSPEL *or* www.regalbooks.com.

Revised edition. *Beyond the Veil* was originally published in 1996 by SpiriTruth Publishing.

Cover Design by Barbara Levan Fisher
Interior Design by Britt Rocchio
Edited by Karen Kaufman

**Library of Congress Cataloging-in-Publication Data**
Smith, Alice
    Beyond the veil / Alice Smith.
        p.        cm.
    ISBN 0-8307-2070-7 (trade paper)
    1. Intercessory prayer—Christianity. I. Title.
    BV210.2.S59     1997                  97-33487
    248.3 2—dc21                       CIP

24 25 26 27 28 29 30 31 32 / 14 13 12 11 10 09

Rights for publishing this book in other languages are contracted by Gospel Light Worldwide, the international nonprofit ministry of Gospel Light. Gospel Light Worldwide also provides publishing and technical assistance to international publishers dedicated to producing Sunday School and Vacation Bible School curricula and books in the languages of the world. For additional information, visit www.gospellightworldwide.org; write to Gospel Light Worldwide, P.O. Box 3875, Ventura, CA 93006; or send an e-mail to info@gospellightworldwide.org.write to Gospel Light Worldwide, P.O. Box 3875, Ventura, CA 93006; or send an e-mail to info@gospellightworldwide.org.

As a tribute to the past,
and in anticipation of the future,
I affectionately dedicate this book to my husband,
Eddie, my partner in the ministry.

## In Loving Memory...

of my sister, Martha Jean Hallmark, who died on Resurrection Day, April 7, 1996. Martha Jean was full of enthusiastic joy, even to the end. With her infectious laugh, and sparkling personality, she displayed for all to see what the apostle James meant when he said, "Consider it pure joy, my brothers [and sisters], whenever you face trials of many kinds" (Jas. 1:2).

# Contents

# Foreword

We who are living today have the privilege of living in the midst of the greatest worldwide prayer movement that Christianity has ever known. Check it out with any church historian. Never before have so many people from so many different Christian traditions, in so many places, and using such creative methods been praying so intensely and so long. They are praying inside their churches, in their homes and out in their communities. Some outdoor sports stadiums are being filled with tens of thousands of believers for literal all-night prayer meetings.

As a predictable part of this prayer phenomenon, which seems to be increasing in magnitude on almost a monthly basis, a high profile corps of specially gifted prayer leaders has been emerging. Reflecting on almost five decades of moving in Christian leadership circles, I cannot remember when, in the past, lists of the most influential Christian leaders would include those whose major contribution to the Body of Christ was prayer ministry. Today such a list would be regarded as poorly informed if such names did not appear on it. The usual evangelists, pastors, executives, missionaries, authors and scholars are now joined by "pray-ers" as high visibility role models for the Church.

What makes this ironic is that individuals with the gift of intercession ordinarily do not want to be up front. Their major service to God is in the closet, not on the platform, and they are happiest in the secret place with their Father. By definition, however, movements have leaders and we are now blessed with increasing numbers of closet people who are also at home on the platform.

Alice Smith is one of these individuals. She has been a central figure in the lives of my wife, Doris, and me for many years. It began during one of those rare, but exhilarating, occasions, clearly orchestrated by God, in which previous strangers bond almost instantaneously and begin a lifetime relationship. Alice tells the story, which took place in Yonggi Cho's church in Seoul, Korea, later in this book. I tell it from my perspective, in my book *Prayer Shield* (Regal Books). The upshot was that Doris and I later invited Alice to serve God, and us, as our I-1 intercessor. Ever since, she has been faithfully standing in the gap on our behalf.

For 10 years now, prayer has been my principal area of research, writing and teaching. I have developed a measure of professional competence in the field, not as an intercessor per se, but as an interpreter and coordinator of the world prayer movement. I display this credential in order to give credibility to this statement: *Beyond the Veil* is a book that is one of a kind. Unprecedented numbers of excellent books about prayer are now available. However, none that I know of takes us so sensitively into the mind and heart of a bona fide intercessor.

If you have ever joined me in asking the question: What is it that makes these intercessors tick? you will love this book.

As you turn these pages you will frequently hear the voice of God. For some this book will bring insight and discovery. For others, however, it will evoke a divine call to a lifetime in the ranks of those whom God desires to take *Beyond the Veil!*

C. Peter Wagner
Fuller Theological Seminary
Colorado Springs, Colorado

# Acknowledgments

~~~

My football-coach daddy would tell me, "Alice Lee, I don't care how many times you fail, just don't ever give up!" I cannot begin to tell you how many times I wanted to "give up" on this book. However, I have both my earthly father and my heavenly Father to thank for not doing so.

I am especially grateful to my husband, Eddie, for the honor and respect he shows to those who devote their lives to prayer. For all the years you survived my endless questions, sleepless nights, uncontrolled tears and radical acts of obedience, God bless you, Eddie. No words in the English language could ever express my gratitude for the many hours you have spent encouraging, reading and editing this book. I love you.

To my children, Robert, Julie, Bryan and Ashlee, who were instruments of God's grace as they released me to the closet for prayer and writing. To Ashlee, our youngest child: You have given up so much to allow me the time to write this book. You knew how important this was to me. I pray the Lord will impart to you a double portion of the mantle of intercession, for you, Ashlee, live in crucial days of humanity.

To my mother, Martha Day, and my father, the late Gene Day: Thank you for 51 years of loving each other, and faithfully taking us to the house of God.

To my father-in-law, Robert Smith: You are a splendid example of what Jesus would look like if He were on the earth today.

To Peter and Doris Wagner: Thank you for your reassurance that one day this book would be a reality. You are truly "spiritual parents" to so many of us. Only heaven knows the personal sacrifices you both make.

To my older sister, JoAnn McDougal: You are a support for our family. Because of you, we are all stronger.

To my brother, John Day: God used you as the tool to teach me how to fast, travail, persevere, fight and believe Him for victory. Every time I see you, I know the power of answered prayer.

To Houston House of Prayer and the U.S. Prayer Track, Houston, Texas, for your selfless sacrifice of prayer and ministry to the whole Body of Christ nationwide.

Many thanks to:

Kyle Duncan: Regal is blessed to have you as their associate publisher. You believed in this message and I am grateful for your continual encouragement.

Karen Kaufman: Thank you for editing this book for me. You are a diamond out of whom brilliant rays of God's glory shine. You light up my life.

Anne Money: For challenging me to finish the work that God had begun in me. I cannot begin to express how much I appreciate everything you have done to help with the completion of this book.

Glen Becker: You have a unique ability to know when to add, or take away from the text of a chapter. Thanks for your devotion to this project.

Tammy Ross: I must give you credit for reading the book, and helping me overcome my frustration.

Sehoy Meeks: I appreciate your expertise in editing. Given to the smallest detail, your help was invaluable.

To all my intercessors: With your labor of prayer and God's divine mercy, it is finished!

To my heavenly Bridegroom, Jesus Christ: You are the Apple of my eye, the Joy in my heart, and my Best Friend. It is my great pleasure to be your Bride.

# CHAPTER ONE

# Can You Hear the Call?

## FACE THE FACTS!

It was a beautiful fall day—a perfect time to curl up in a chair and read the mountains of journals that had been accumulating on the floor of my den. Fully appreciating the break from all responsibility, I felt relaxed and carefree. I had just completed a magazine when as I glanced down at the next journal in the stack, I was jolted by its horrific headline: "Killer Kids: An American Tragedy." I could feel my stomach tighten as I picked up the journal and opened it to the featured article.

My heart began to race when I read, "Fourteen-year-old Eric Smith was convicted of bludgeoning 4-year-old Derrick Robie to death. His lawyer attempted to prove the teen's innocence, saying the reason for his action was a mental disease—intermittent explosive disorder, which causes eruptions of uncontrollable rage. Eric was sentenced to a maximum prison term of nine years to life."[1] Stunned, tears flowed down my cheeks as I found my way into the prayer closet, knowing the only answer for the decadence of our society is a divine visitation of almighty God.

Our society is reaching the depths of decay and degradation. Abortion, murder, suicide and war ravage every continent. As Kay Arthur, outstanding Bible scholar and vice president of Precepts Ministries recently said, "America's cup of iniquity is full." Not only that, but hunger, starvation and disasters abound.

Our world is in a state of chaos. Society is being destroyed by its own evil devices.

We are foolish to think we can solve these problems ourselves. Contrary to popular belief, education is not the answer to AIDS, drug abuse, crime, premarital sex nor the many other ills of our world. The time has come for us to admit that we are helpless! Many of our best plans, including many plans of the Church, have failed.

In the spring of 1995, Oprah Winfrey introduced Families for a Better Life. Her aim was to give poor urban families $30,000 a year for a two-year period, along with education or job training, health care and counseling. She also pledged to donate an additional $6 million and hoped to enlist corporate sponsors to continue the precedent she had set.

Although Winfrey's motives were benevolent and one might think this kind of giving would reduce crime, statistics prove that giving welfare is an ineffective means for conquering the problem. A survey of the U.S. Department of Justice in 1991 revealed that while welfare spending increased by 800 percent, the crime rate tripled. Who has the answer?

## POWERLESS, PRAYERLESS AND PURPOSELESS

The Church *has* the answer! The answer is the presence and power of God expressed through an intimate relationship with Jesus Christ. But many in the Church seek His *presents* rather than His *presence*. They seek the *power of God* rather than relationship with the *God of power*. The Church is generally *powerless*. We can no longer say, as Peter said, "Silver or gold I do not have, but what I have I give you. In the name of Jesus Christ of Nazareth, walk" (Acts 3:6). When the world needs us most, sin, division and faithlessness have left us impotent.

We are unable to do the works Jesus did, let alone the greater things He claimed we would and could do. He told us that "anyone who has faith in me will do what I have been doing. He will do even greater things than these, because I am going to the Father" (John 14:12). So why aren't we doing them?

The apostle Paul could say, "My message and my preaching

were not with wise and persuasive words, but with a demonstration of the Spirit's power" (1 Cor. 2:4). Yet, we must pitifully beg the world to believe us for our word's sake. We aren't doing His works because many believers are too out of touch with God to allow the Spirit to display His power!

Perhaps the Church's strength is its own greatest weakness. Refined and rigid, the Church has assessed, prioritized, planned and prayed with superficial consideration for God to *bless* its plan. Strangely, we have overlooked a powerful key to the ministry of Jesus, who said, "I tell you the truth, the Son can do nothing by himself; he can do only what he sees his Father doing, because whatever the Father does the Son also does" (John 5:19). Jesus had power for ministry because He had an intimate relationship with the Father. We must discover what is on God's heart and join Him! Only by praying intimately are we able to discover what He is doing. "Surely the Lord God does nothing, unless He reveals His secret to His servants" (Amos 3:7, *NKJV*).

Our powerlessness is largely a result of our *prayerlessness*. We are eating the bitter fruit of prayerlessness and our children, government, churches and society are reaping the result of dry eyes in the pews and crusty hearts in the pulpits. Ed Silvoso says it well in his book *That None Should Perish*:

> When Christians begin to pray for the felt needs of the lost, God surprises them with almost immediate answers to prayer. In fact, prayer for the needs of that one-hundredth sheep is the spiritual equivalent of dialing 911.[2]

Another problem is our commitment level. Not only are we prayerless, but we are also *purposeless*. Rather than a commitment to reach the world with the gospel, most of us are satisfied to attend weekly services. Too often they are "weakly" services. Where is the "salt" in our society? Jesus said, "You are the salt of the earth. But if the salt loses its saltiness, how can it be made salty again? It is no longer good for anything, except to be thrown out and trampled by men" (Matt. 5:13).

Salt that has lost its saltiness (or flavor) takes on the taste of the food with which it is mixed. Ironically, the Church has taken on "the flavor of the world." As someone has said, "We are good, but we are good for nothing!" We are not willing to die for Christ, much less lay down our lives for one another.

My husband Eddie's father, Robert E. Smith, is an example of one who was willing to lay down his life for others. He not only demonstrated purpose but also commitment. For years, Eddie and I watched as Dad and Mom would pay their bills, then cash the remainder of their paycheck and drive into Northern Mexico to share their money with several struggling Mexican pastors. Robert—we call him Dad—has faithfully pastored several churches, was president of the Valley Baptist Academy (a secondary school for Latin American children), served as chairman of the Southern Baptist Foreign Mission Board and for more than 17 years was area missionary for the Rio Grande Valley of Texas.

When Eddie's mother passed away recently, I spent one afternoon reading hundreds of beautiful expressions of love for both Robert and Marguerite Smith sent by their friends.

I will never forget one letter in particular. It was from Paul Powell, president of the Annuity Board for the Southern Baptist Convention. Many years ago, Paul was the pastor of Green Acres Baptist Church in Tyler, Texas. Each summer, churches bring busloads of people to the Valley for mission trips. (I know because I was in a youth group that went one summer.) Dad would take them across the border into Mexico. Paul Powell's church was one of them. In his letter to Dad he said,

> *I remember the first visit with Dr. Smith at Diaz Ordaz, Mexico. You (Robert) stopped before we got to the International Bridge and said, "I want to warn you, once you see the ignorance and spiritual darkness of this city, you are as responsible as I am for doing something about it. Do you still want to go?"*
>
> *That made a lasting impression on me. I shall never forget it and will forever be indebted to you for it.*

(You will be blessed to know that Paul Powell acted on what he saw. He understood the purpose and responsibility of the Church. He went back to the church he pastored and raised more than $40,000, of which $20,000 helped to build a Hispanic Baptist Church in Mexico. The other $20,000 was given to the mission fund of the Southern Baptist Convention. This was twice the money that Paul's church had ever given to missions.)

## UNITED WE STAND—DIVIDED WE FALL

Not only are we *powerless, prayerless* and *purposeless*, but we are also *polarized, pulled apart* and *pitted against each other*. Division is reducing the Church's effectiveness by causing it to operate in a spirit of dysfunction, disharmony and disillusionment.

> *Why should the lost world have faith in us when we do not have confidence in God or each other?*

Jesus warned us about this when He said, "Every kingdom divided against itself will be ruined, and every city or household divided against itself will not stand" (Matt. 12:25). The city of Zion and the household of God are divided. Christian brothers and sisters are arguing over minor doctrinal issues and complaining about services that linger past noon while men, women and young people from every nation slip hopelessly into eternal hell.

Christ is the only solution to this counterproductive grumbling and bickering. He gave us the perfect example of unity by showing us the relationship between the Father and Himself. The intimacy of this Father and Son relationship is revealed throughout Scripture. Christ said, "I in them and you in me. May they be brought to *complete unity* to let the world know that you sent me and have loved them even as you have loved me" (John 17:23, italics added). Our world doesn't believe us! Why? Because we are not one with Jesus Christ and we are not one with each other. Why should the lost world have faith in us when we do not have confidence in God or each other? We must be willing to imitate the unity Christ and the Father have modeled for us if we are to successfully build His Kingdom.

At the building of the Tower of Babel, the Lord explained, "If *as one people* speaking the same language they have begun to do this, then *nothing* they plan to do will be impossible for them" (Gen. 11:6, italics added).

Satan has learned this lesson well. Satanists defend witches while abortionists support gay rights and vice versa. When will the Church grasp what the Father said? When will we begin to stand with each other across denominational and cultural lines as one person, Christ's Bride, for the intention of God?

## LINKING HEARTS AND HANDS

A recent news broadcast reported about a little boy who wandered away from his family in a state park. After a couple of days of air searches, an alert was released encouraging people to come to the park for a final sweep. Thousands of caring people came together on the campgrounds and received instruction. As directed, they clasped hands and formed a single line hundreds of yards wide. They walked slowly through the wooded area. In almost no time the search ended. There, in a small ravine where he had curled up in the cold of the night, lay the dead body of the tiny boy. The grief-stricken father's response was sobering. He simply said, "If only we had taken hands sooner, my boy might still be alive."

Is this what a grief-stricken heavenly Father will say to us? "If only you had taken hands sooner, millions would not have slipped into outer darkness."

Unity comes when we link hearts and hands in prayer to partner with the heavenly Father in His plan and purpose for saving the lost. And *when we are prayerless, we are powerless.* Overcomers are developed in the prayer closet. The more time we invest at His feet, the longer we will be able to stand as a whole (unified) Body empowered and charged with God's energy and authority to trample the enemy under our own feet.

We must remember that behind divisions in the Church are spiritual forces of darkness that can only be pulled down through prayer. Paul wrote, "For our struggle is not against flesh and blood, but against the rulers, against the authorities, against the powers of this dark world and against the spiritual forces of evil in the heavenly realms" (Eph. 6:12). This conquering authority for the Church is found in prayer. Let me say it again: *The person who is prayerless is powerless.*

## CHOSEN TO PARTNER

But those who *do* pray are united with the Father as partners in bringing about His purposes and plans on earth. Through prayer the Church is empowered to be salt and light in this troubled world. God has chosen to include us as His partners. This partnership, however, is based on daily intimate prayer. Thus, it is the unfamiliarity of relating to our heavenly Bridegroom (see John 3:29), who knows all and can do anything, that sometimes robs us of our privilege to partner with Him.

We *can* learn of Him by building relationship with Him. And that relationship is formed as we invest intimate times of listening, learning to trust through obedience to His Word and living in oneness with Him—abiding in Him. "If you remain [abide] in me and my words remain [abide] in you, ask whatever you wish, and it will be given you" (John 15:7). The Lord will entrust the powerful things of His Kingdom to those who have found an abiding place in Him.

Some wrongly assume that what the Father is going to do, He will do with or without us. Right? Wrong! We are God's chosen partners. Need I remind you of Joshua's battle in Exodus 17? Moses told Joshua to go fight the Amalekites while he lifted his hands as a token of victory. As long as Moses' hands were lifted, God enabled Joshua's army to win. When Moses' hands began to drop, so Joshua's men began to drop. Listen! This was life and death! These sons and dads were dying. Spears were being driven through their bellies and arrows were piercing their hearts.

It was a critical moment. Moses didn't say, "Well, if God

wants our army to win, it will. He doesn't need me. I am too inadequate to be used of God this way. After all, He is not only sovereign, He is also omnipotent. He will use someone else to do it." No!

Aaron and Hur were summoned into duty until the battle was won, knowing that holding up the hands of their leader, Moses, meant life or death for others! After the victory was secured, Moses built an altar and called it, "The Lord is my Banner. He said, 'For hands were lifted up to the throne of the Lord'" (Exod. 17:15,16). Obediently holding up the hands of others, especially our leaders, is our responsibility as believers!

### WHY, LORD?

Rather than being instantly obedient, however, we often sit around wanting to know why. For example, God has told us the importance of *persistence* in prayer. He is the One who said to

*The more we know Him,*
*the more we love Him.*
*Hopelessly in love with Him,*
*our goals are lost in His.*

keep on asking and you will keep on receiving, keep on knocking and it will keep on being opened to you, keep on seeking and you will keep on finding (see Luke 11:9,10). Yet I often hear people teach that to ask God for something more than once is unbelief. If this teaching were correct, why would Jesus have declared, "Pray always and do not faint" (see Luke 18:1-8)?

Kay Arthur recently told the following wonderful story that illustrates how perseverance works to bring us to a place of intimacy in prayer:

My husband Jack and I were watching a medical program on television one night. They showed an open heart surgery. Two human hearts were laying side by side. Each was beating at different rhythms. The surgeon moved them together, until the tissue of one heart touched the other. Suddenly, both assumed the same rhythm."[3]

This is an amazing picture of intimacy. As our hearts touch the Father's heart, we assume the same rhythm, the same desires and the same goals. The more we know Him, the more we love Him. Hopelessly in love with Him, our goals are lost in His.

His burden becomes the focus of our intercession. We begin to see issues as He sees them. Our hearts become united with His. The hungering heart that burns with desire for intimate communion will be enabled by the Holy Spirit to taste the joys of heaven and experience the ecstasy of seeing many people prayed into the kingdom of God.

## INTERCESSION IS THE KEY

C. Peter Wagner said that in the decade of the 1980s we saw the restoration of the prophetic ministry, and in the 1990s we are seeing the restoration of intercession. Regarding the prophetic purposes of God, and the desperate need of humanity, this generation cries out for intercessors in the house of prayer! This despairing generation cries out for people who know their God intimately!

But many do not bother to develop intimacy because they are not convinced that their prayer will make a difference. Perhaps you too are wondering: *To what extent does God honor our prayers?* That question can best be answered by observing what God has done through the intercession of others. Let's consider one of the great revivals in American history.

In October 1976, James Edwin Orr presented a lecture in Dallas, Texas, giving the account of the Great Revival of 1800 in America. He described the deplorable conditions of the society, both secular and sacred:

There was an unprecedented moral slump following

the American Revolution (1775-1783). Drunkenness was epidemic. Out of a population of 5 million, there were 300,000 confirmed drunkards. Profanity was of the most shocking kind. For the first time in the history of the American settlement, women were afraid to be out at night. Bank robberies were a daily occurrence.[4]

In 1794, conditions reached their worst. Of course, dire circumstances never open the illimitable resources of heaven, but prayer does. A Baptist minister, Isaac Backus, known as much for his praying as for his exhorting, had an encounter with the Holy Spirit. The impression left upon him was: *There's only one power on earth that commands the power of heaven—prayer.*[5]

He wrote "Plea for Prayer for Revival of Religion" and mailed it to ministers of every denomination in the United States, pleading each pastor to set aside the first Monday of each month as a time to open his church all day in order to conduct extraordinary prayer for revival. As a result, people humbled themselves and began to cry out to the Lord. God poured upon them the spirit of supplication. (Burning, believing, prevailing, persuading, persevering, intimate prayer always precedes a move of God.)

## FANNING THE FLAMES OF REVIVAL

The intercession of Backus and those who joined him fanned the fires of revival during 1798 in New England. Churches were unable to accommodate those inquiring about salvation. Multitudes were won to the Lord. As the flames of revival were fanned, new fires were kindled.

By July 1800, unprecedented numbers began arriving in Cane Ridge, Kentucky. A multitude estimated at 11,000 flocked to this camp meeting. (The largest city in Kentucky was Lexington, which had a population of only 1,800!) James McGready, a staid Presbyterian pastor from Pennsylvania, described the scene in the following words:

The cries of the distressed arose almost as loud as [Methodist pastor] McGee's voice. Here awakening and converting work was to be found in every part of the multitude, and even some things strangely and wonderfully new to me.⁶

The Cane Ridge Camp Meeting of 1800 brought a change to the spiritual face of the United States. Thousands upon thousands of souls came into the Kingdom.

One humble, desperate Baptist minister, Isaac Backus, had called for a national day of prayer for revival each week and from this humble call, revival swept across all denominational and racial barriers!

Let's retrace the steps of this revival:

- First, a solitary man had an encounter with the Holy Spirit.
- Second, a solitary man initiated the effort.
- Third, a united prayer emphasis developed.
- Fourth, revival came!

Revival begins in the prayer closet! It happens as a result of intercession!

I am convinced that the reason so few accept God's call to intimate intercession is that we do not understand His original purpose nor are we committed to it. We are so busy living out our own agendas that we are unwilling to take the time to get to know Him intimately. And it is only out of an intimate relationship that intercession will flow.

When we get serious about prayer, then the tears, fasting and travail of intercession will cause the golden bowls of incense in heaven to overflow:

Each one had a harp and they were holding golden bowls full of incense, which are the prayers of the saints (Rev. 5:8).

Another angel, who had a golden censer, came and stood at the altar. He was given much incense to offer, with the prayers of all the saints, on the golden altar before the throne. The smoke of the incense, together

with the prayers of the saints, went up before God from
the angel's hand (Rev. 8:3,4).

In the unseen heavenlies, before the throne of God, the
prayers of the saints rise as incense to the Father and He smells
the sweetness of their cries.

Our prayers coupled with the Father's great unlimited compassion for His children will set into motion the greatest out-
pouring of His Spirit the world has ever seen.

Time is fleeting! Earnestly ask the Lord to fan the flames of
passionate love for Him in your life as you enter the Promised
Land of intercession. Your life will never be the same! Eternity is
at stake! Listen to the voice of the Bridegroom. He is calling you!
He loves you! Jesus longs to fellowship with you! His heart is full
of secrets that He is wanting to tell you now. "The Lord confides
in those who fear him; he makes his covenant known to them"
(Ps. 25:14). Hear Him today!

## A WINDOW OF OPPORTUNITY

Those who have been remiss about prayer can start today. God is
giving us another chance. This may well be our last chance. The
Holy Spirit is stirring up what is already the greatest prayer
movement in the history of the Church!

George Otis, Jr. stated in his book, *The Last of the Giants*:

As the Church proceeds toward the year 2000, no other
reminder is more appropriate to the occasion.
Multitudes still wait in the valley of decision: the question is simply who will reach them first? Never before
has the competition for souls been so fierce. Never
before has the Church had to contend with such a
diverse assortment of rivals so utterly committed to the
principles of activism. Fortunately, it is into just such an
hour that God has promised through the prophet Joel to
pour out His Spirit upon all flesh.[7]

There are 180 million Christians worldwide committed to

praying for global revival and the completion of the Great Commission. Twenty million report that intercession is their primary calling.

World prayer is now focusing on unreached people. Ninety-seven percent of the world's neediest reside in the 65 nations of what is known as the 10/40 Window—an imaginary rectangle that stretches from the 10th to the 40th parallel north, and extends from Spain to Japan. The goal of the A.D. 2000 and Beyond Movement was "A Church for every people and the gospel for every person by the year 2000!" There *are* signs of revival! There *are* signs of unity! The Father *is* calling the Bride to be one with His Son!

The door of intimacy is open to all those who will enter. The Lord delights in the believer who, yearning to know what cannot be known naturally, enters the Holy of Holies through prayer with simplicity and humility. Beyond this veil, which formerly separated us from the Holy of Holies (see Matt. 27:51; Heb. 9:3, *NKJV*), the child of God will touch the heart of God, bask in His loving words of affirmation, tremble at His unlimited power and authority, and come away forever changed. If we do not enter in, the problem does not lie with the Lord withholding from His Bride—the problem is that we are unwilling to "lose all to gain Christ."

UNVEILING THE TRUTH ABOUT YOU

1. Do you agree that the Church has been powerless, prayerless and purposeless? In which of these areas do you struggle most? What steps are you willing to take to bring about change?
2. Is unity a priority in your life? What is the heart of the Father regarding the issue of unity? (See John 17:23.) As much as it's up to you, how will you bring unity to the Church?
3. Is prayer a priority in your life? Have you found yourself *doing for* God instead of *being with* God? How has this affected the depth of intimacy you now experience in prayer?

4. In what ways does revival need to occur in you? in your family? in your church? in your city? in your nation? What price will you pay to bring it about?

## Notes

1. Rosaline Bush, "America Mourns: Children Who Kill," *Family Voice*, 17, no. 1 (January 1995): 6.
2. Ed Silvoso, *That None Should Perish* (Ventura, Calif.: Regal Books, 1995), p. 84.
3. Kay Arthur delivering a speech in Orlando, Florida during "The Special Call to Prayer and Fasting in America" sponsored by Bill Bright and Campus Crusade for Christ, December 5-7, 1994.
4. Mary Stewart Relfe, Ph.D., "Cure of All Ills" (Montgomery, Ala.: League of Prayers, Copy Permission Granted), May 24, 1994.
5. Ibid.
6. Ibid.
7. George Otis, Jr., *The Last of the Giants* (Tarryton, N.Y.: Chosen Books, 1991), p. 252.

# CHAPTER TWO

# A Higher Purpose

## BRIDGING THE GAP

One night a little boy was overheard praying, "Jesus, take care of my daddy and my mommy. Also take care of sister Jane, and my baby brother, Bobby. And take care of my puppy, Snuggles. Oh, by the way Jesus, take care of Yourself...if something were to happen to You, we'd all be in a mess!"

Yes we would all be in a mess! For it is God Almighty choosing to interface with us through prayer and intercession that offers us hope in this desperate hour. And because intimate intercession is the answer, why is so little of it being done? What is prayer and how does it differ from intercession?

## GOING BETWEEN

Webster defines "prayer" as "the act of asking for a favor with earnestness." He defines "intercession" as "pleading in favor of another." "Intercession" is derived from the Latin word *inter*, meaning "between," and *cedere*, meaning "to go." So intercession means "to go between." We often think of intercession as synonymous with prayer.

In his book *Prayer Shield*, Peter Wagner says, "We use the terms interchangeably. However, technically they are very different. Prayer generally means speaking, to request, to talk, to commune, to fellowship, to offer petition, and supplication. Intercession on the other hand means coming to God on the behalf of another."[1]

Intercession involves the whole spirit, soul and body. And when the Father gives us intercessory burdens, each of these areas in our lives will be affected. To prepare we must:

• Desire to work toward a disciplined life;
• Pursue a regular prayer time;
• Maintain a clear conscience;
• Be willing to partner with God for the needs of others;
• Be willing to obey instantly.

Paul said to the Colossians, "We always thank God,...when we pray for you...For this reason, since the day we heard about you, we have not stopped praying for you...I labor, struggling with all his energy, which so powerfully works in me" (1:3,9,29). The word translated "to labor" is *kopiao*. It means "to toil, to become weary or to be fatigued." The word translated "struggling" is the Greek word *agonizomai*, meaning "to agonize, to fight or to contend against." Paul was describing something more than prayer. He was *laboring in travail* for the power of God to dispel works of darkness.

Intercession can literally order or change the course of a nation, a city, a family or a church. It is neither "emotional hype," rituals, prayer lists, nor obligations. It is a Spirit-led privilege. Magnificent and wonderful revelations have come because of prayer and intercession. These revelations are the result of intimate fellowship with the Lord.

## GOD SPEAKS *TO* AND *THROUGH* INTERCESSORS

Our former church in Houston, Texas, had sent a missionary to Latvia (a Baltic state of the former Soviet Union). A team from our church was invited there to provide instruction about lay ministry. During our visit to Latvia in 1992, I felt the Lord speak to me in one of the prayer meetings held every Monday evening for the American missionaries who live in Latvia.

On that snowy November night, about 15 of us (some whom we did not know) nestled together in a small apartment rented by our American missionary. Stillness had settled over the room as the praise and worship concluded. Unexpectedly, I heard the Lord speak softly in my mind. The Lord told me that the American missionary sitting across the room was scheduled to make a proposal to a high-ranking Latvian official the next day. I felt the Holy Spirit say that what this missionary wanted to propose to this government official was of the Lord. I was compelled to tell him this message!

I asked the Lord, "Are you sure this is right? Lord, I don't even know this man and You want me to tell him something this extraordinary?" I took comfort in what John and Paula Sanford say in their book *Elijah Task*, "Though our freedom to fail is not to be used by us as license to escape from responsibility, a part of a prophet's sanity-saving armor is the happy knowledge that if he [or she] goofs, God is big enough to take care of it."[2] I was praying the Lord would cover my "goofs" in this situation. And so without further instruction, I gingerly walked across the room to this stranger and asked if he would let me pray for him.

The missionary, Larry Stout, nodded affirmatively. Placing my hand on his head, I tentatively started to pray for him under my breath. After delaying as long as I could, I leaned over and began speaking the message I believe the Lord had given me.

"Sir, I believe the Lord was speaking to me about you just a minute ago. He told me you are going to be having a meeting with a very important government official of the Latvian government tomorrow."

Immediately, he put his hand on top of mine and began to weep softly, shaking his head with a yes. (I can't tell you how relieved I was to see this.)

I continued, "I also believe the Lord said there is something in your heart you really want to share with this official, but you are unsure if it is from God. The Lord said to tell you that this revelation *is* from Him and you are to go with success."

When we finished praying, I learned that Larry Stout is a missionary and educator from Pennsylvania. He had an appointment with the Latvian president the next day to review his proposal for teaching Judeo-Christian literature in Latvian schools. Larry wanted to add a clause proposing that Latvia establish a National Day of Prayer, but he was unsure if this was God's idea or his own. As

I confirmed what the Lord was saying, Larry was very excited!

At the meeting the next day, the president agreed to use the curriculum and to establish a National Day of Prayer. The first National Day of Prayer in Latvia was May 29, 1993. Hallelujah!

Encouragement was given to a brother because *revelation* was imparted during intercession. Understanding the word "revelation," at best, can be difficult. Cindy Jacobs, in her book *The Voice of God*, explains, "I am aware that the way I use the word 'revelation' may be disturbing to some sectors of the Church. The word 'revelation' is used here not to refer in the technical sense to the words of Scripture. 'Revelation' is used here in the broader sense of the word in such passages as Matthew 11:27; Romans 1:18; 1 Corinthians 14:30; Ephesians 1:17 and Philippians 3:15 to refer to communication and prophetic words from God that are not equal in authority to Scripture."[3]

Revelation can come from three sources:

- The Holy Spirit;
- The enemy; or
- Our soul.

Never assume you are right about everything you hear. God gives us revelation to feed our prayers, not our egos! Even the apostle Paul said, "Now we see but a poor reflection as in a mirror" (1 Cor. 13:12). "For we know in part and we prophesy in part" (v. 9). Rather than saying for certain what God *is* saying, exercise the discipline, when you can, of sharing with others what you think God *may* be saying. Ask the Lord to confirm what you think He has said.

Do not be offended at the idea that your revelation might have come from an active imagination or from last night's pizza! No one is right all the time! Relax, risk and free yourself from the need to be right every time. But remember to check your motives.

Because an intercessor is likely to receive more revelation than many others in the Body of Christ, the temptation can be to think that this revelation qualifies us for a "spiritual badge." Not true. Revelation is a sacred honor! Being privy to spiritual knowledge places us in a position of greater responsibility to pray for others and greater accountability to God.

I believe intercessors who have developed a close relationship with Jesus Christ have learned to be trustworthy with the information God shares with them. They have learned to hold 80 percent of what they receive from the Lord and reveal only 20 percent. Most of the revelation they receive never leaves the prayer closet. As partners with God, intercessors are in a place of hiddenness. They must depend upon the Holy Spirit for discernment for what, how much and when to share.

When is it right to reveal revelation? Let's look at three basic guidelines:

1. Words of encouragement: exhortation, affirmation and blessings are a "green light." Deliver them joyfully.
2. Words of warning: correction or rebuke is considered a "yellow light." Deliver the word only after you have received confirmation and then, cautiously.
3. Words of judgment: destruction, despair, doom and chastisement are a "red light." Stop! Deliver them obediently, only by God's direction! Remember, "in the multitude of counselors there is safety" (see Prov. 11:14, *KJV*) and the prophet is subject to the prophets (see 1 Cor. 14:32, *KJV*). These kinds of words need to be subjected to pastoral leadership before being released.

"Intercession is prayer, but not all prayer is intercession," states Cindy Jacobs in *Possessing the Gates of the Enemy*.[4]

Peter Wagner tells us, in his book *Prayer Shield*, "Theologically, intercession is the act of pleading by one whom in God's sight has the right to do so, to go before Him in order to obtain mercy for someone who is in need."[5]

James gives us the basis for pleading the case of another who is in need. James 2:13 declares, "Mercy triumphs over judgment!" Why does the intercessor ask for mercy?

PENETRATING THE PIT WITH PRAYER

Mercy is at the heart of all God does. We are most like God when we are merciful.

Several years ago, Eddie and I went to a citywide prayer meeting for pastors and prayer leaders. For our prayer time, the director asked us to divide into groups according to the section of town in which we lived. Our group consisted of 15 people, the majority of whom were pastors. A woman began to pray, "And dear Lord, please reverse the curse on the Satanists in our area. May they fall into their own pit."

I was stunned, appalled, shocked and upset! After what seemed like eternity, I began to pray, "Father, thank You that although we deserve judgment, You have offered us mercy. I truly pray that the mercy of God is given to each Satanist in our area of town. May they experience Your unconditional love from some Christian crossing their paths. Bring salvation into their lives and praise into their mouths."

Believe it or not, this lady resumed with the same kind of manipulative and controlling prayer. We should be careful not to pray our own wills and agendas on someone else. Many pastors are discouraged, frustrated and confused because their church members are praying witchcraft-type prayers over them instead of prayers that reinforce God's will and God's kingdom in their lives.

Intercession is the act of standing in the gap between the need we see and the provision of God that we long to see. It can pertain to the need of a person, a church, a city or a nation. Although the Father does not need us to complete His plan for the ages, He continues to call us to participate in its fulfillment. I am convinced He allows us to participate in His plan because He still wants an intimate relationship with us, and the primary way to facilitate that intimacy is through intercession.

The Old Testament provides many examples of intercession. For example, Moses interceded for the nation of Israel and the people were spared (see Exodus 32 and 34). Nehemiah was ordained by God to intercede, then unite the people and rebuild the wall in Jerusalem (see Nehemiah). Anna "served God with fastings and prayers night and day" (Luke 2:37, *KJV*), looking for the Lord who would bring redemption.

The following is an outstanding description of the work of intercession from Job 33:19-30. Read and study these Scriptures carefully:

Or a man may be chastened on a bed of pain with constant distress in his bones, so that his very being finds food repulsive and his soul loathes the choicest meal. His flesh wastes away to nothing, and his bones, once hidden, now stick out. His soul draws near to the pit, and his life to the messengers of death. Yet if there is an angel [*malak*—messenger, priest, prophet or ambassador] on his side as a mediator [*luwts*—to interpret or intercede], one out of a thousand, to tell a man what is right for him, to be gracious to him and say, 'Spare him from going down to the pit; I have found a ransom for him'—then his flesh is renewed like a child's; it is restored as in the days of his youth. He prays to God and finds favor with him, he sees God's face and shouts for joy; he is restored by God to his righteous state. Then he comes to men and says, 'I sinned, and perverted what was right, but I did not get what I deserved. He redeemed my soul from going down to the pit, and I will live to enjoy the light. God does all these things to a man—twice, even three times—to turn back his soul from the pit, that the light of life may shine on him.'

## TOUCHED BY THE CRIES OF HIS CHILDREN

Our compassionate, covenant-making God is touched by the cries of His children. God is sovereign and yet as a faithful Father, He enjoys granting our requests. A primary task of the intercessor is to stand in the gap for the lost. We know that it is not God's desire that our neighbors perish without Him. Jesus died on the cross for everyone. Peter reminds us, "The Lord is not slow in keeping his promise, as some understand slowness. He is patient with you, not wanting anyone to perish, but everyone to come to repentance" (2 Pet. 3:9).

This is not to say that our prayers can usurp the free will of another person; instead our prayers can be used to till the spiritual soil so when the seed of God's Word is sown into the unbeliever's life, it will have a greater chance of taking root.

Years ago I was in a Friday prayer meeting with about 75 of

our church members. As we were seeking the Lord for those who needed a touch from Him, the name "Barry" (not his real name) flashed in my mind. I did not know anyone by that name, yet the Lord continued to burn the name in my heart. Finally at a natural break, I asked the group if anyone knew a man by the name of Barry. "Yes," came the urgent response. "Barry and I work together," Thomas answered. "I have been very concerned because he has been extremely depressed lately."

As we divided into small groups, Thomas joined the group I was in so we could pray for Barry. Amazingly, as we prayed, again a flashing vision came to my mind. I saw a man sitting at a desk in complete confusion and depression. We prayed fervently until the sense of rest had descended upon the group. The next afternoon I received a call from Thomas. "Alice, you are not going to believe what happened last night!"

"What?" I asked curiously.

"I called Barry this morning and told him how you had received his name by revelation from God and how we had prayed for his safety." After a long pause, he told me what happened. He said, "Last night Barry was sitting at his desk feeling total despair. Deciding the fight was not worth it, he had determined he would end his life. Suddenly he had a supernatural impression that God was present in the room—that he was not to harm himself and that he would receive answers later. So he went home. I told Barry how Jesus Christ wanted to be the Lord and Savior of his life. He was so open and ready to hear. He asked if he could talk to you. I gave him your number, okay?"

Later that day I received a call from this influential businessman in our city. We rehearsed on the phone all that had taken place the night before. I shared with Barry how Jesus Christ died for his sins and that He desires a relationship with him. Barry couldn't get past the idea that God would have given someone this information. He asked, "But why would God show you this about me?"

"Because He loves you and wants to give eternal life to you," I explained.

It took several days for Barry to receive the revelation that he was lost, separated from God and hopeless apart from the Lord Jesus. But none of us could have known the rest of the story.

Tuesday night after that Friday night prayer meeting, Thomas suffered a heart attack and went to be with the Lord. This was a grievous time for all who had been involved. I called Barry the day before the funeral. With deep sorrow for the loss of his friend, but much more definition about the reality of eternity, our friend "Barry" accepted Christ as his Savior.

I had lost contact with Barry and often wondered where his decision had taken him. Recently, however, one of our prayer partners, Greg, unknowingly chose to sit next to him at a Promise Keepers meeting. After introducing themselves, the two men began sharing the details of how they had become Christians. When Barry mentioned my name, our friend Greg told Barry that he was a friend of mine. With great excitement, Barry spilled out the story you have just read. Barry and his family are faithfully serving the Lord today.

Others had cared enough to pay the price in praying for Barry so Christ could show him the ultimate price that had been paid for his life.

But what happens in the case of those who perish? They slip through the gap. Perhaps it is because someone was unwilling to be the "go between," to pray and to fight the spiritual battle for their souls. Who is standing in the gap for your lost friends and relatives? What prayer price are you willing to pay to see them saved?

History records that Frederick the Great wrote to one of his generals, "I send you with 60,000 men against the enemy." Upon numbering the troops, however, it was found that there were only 50,000. The general expressed surprise at such a mistake on the part of his sovereign. Frederick's reply was, "I counted on you for 10,000 men!" How much time can the Lord Jesus count on from you to pray in the many souls who need to hear the gospel?

INTERCEPTING AND INTERCHANGING
THE ENEMY'S PLANS

Suppose you know a person whose life is being destroyed by sin. You know that this is not God's plan for this person, but what do you do with this information?

*1. Accept the burden from the Lord.* Because the Lord is a gentle-
man, He will never force you to bear a burden unwillingly. He
does, however, offend your mind in order to change your heart
(see 1 Sam. 19:24; Mic. 1:8). The Lord has chosen to partner with
each of us so that together we may see the Great Commission fulfilled. But when we will not participate, He will find another:

> He saw that there was no one, he was appalled that
> there was no one to intervene; so his own arm worked
> salvation for him, and his own righteousness sustained
> him (Isa. 59:16).

The Lord often communicates His burden to intercessors
through what I call "triggers." These prompts or triggers for
intercession come in many forms. Sometimes, for no apparent
reason, you may sense a very strong *heaviness* coming over you
(see Matt. 11:28-30). In your mind you know you are not in sin,
the family is fine, and yet that heaviness remains over you. This
is the Lord's way of saying "go pray."

At other times a deep, *overwhelming desire to weep* affects you
(see Rom. 8:26). Again, this comes suddenly and for no known
reason. The Lord is asking you to slip away and intercede for
something or somebody. Most of the time He will not give you
the second step until you have taken the first step.

I'm amazed at the number of emotionally and mentally
depressed Christians who take antidepressant medications. I
believe many of these "depressed Christians" are receiving a
"trigger" call to intercede.

Other triggers God uses to get our attention to pray include:

- A mental picture (see Acts 21:10,11) of something or
  someone that flashes into your mind;
- An intense longing to be alone with God (see Ps.
  42:1,2);
- A dream (see Acts 2:17,18);
- A physical weakness such as Daniel experienced (see
  Dan. 8:17,18,27);
- A dull heartache (see Rom. 9:2);
- A burning in the pit of the stomach (see Luke 24:32);

- A sensation of feeling flushed (see Isa. 40:29-31);
- A small, quiet voice in your mind saying to pray (see Matt. 14:23; Luke 6:12);
- A sense of emergency (see Daniel 7:15); and
- A flash of a name or face across your mind (see Acts 9:10-14).

The next time any of these triggers occurs, be like Samuel, who when he realized it was the Lord speaking to him said, "Speak [Lord], for your servant is listening" (1 Sam. 3:10).

Agree with God in prayer. You might pray, "Father, You have determined that we are to be partners in prayer and that You will act according to my prayer. You want to use me to stand in the gap for something important to You. I agree with Your plan. Send

*P.U.S.H!* Pray Until Something Happens!

Your Holy Spirit to make a way where the enemy has brought spiritual blindness and hindrance. Come with a powerful breakthrough for Your namesake. I know that You are more interested in my 'availability' than my 'ability.' I give myself to You."

2. *Identify with God's desire to intervene.* Once you have accepted the assignment to intercede, recognize that it is His desire to intervene. You are being asked to "stand in the gap" between what the heavenly Father wants and what the enemy is trying to do. Thank the Lord for the opportunity to see the kingdom of darkness replaced by the Kingdom of Light. Exercising priestly authority, ask the Lord to intercept or stop the devil's plan to "kill, steal and destroy" (see John 10:10). Cry out to God for mercy, reminding Him that "mercy triumphs over judgment" (James 2:13).

3. *Intercede by faith for breakthrough.* Pray for God's plan to be established in the person's life. Make sure you are *praying through* instead of *through praying!* The Lord is looking for perseverance

in the prayer closet. Actively stand in faith. "And without faith it is impossible to please God, because anyone who comes to him must believe that he exists and that he rewards those who earnestly seek Him" (Heb. 11:6). Nothing blesses God more than earnest faith. Around our church we have a slogan:

P.U.S.H! Pray Until Something Happens!

Once a breakthrough comes—STOP PRAYING! To press further can lead to unbelief. Let me put it this way, "When the horse dies, dismount!" The burden from the Lord may return later. When it does, this is not a sign of unbelief, but a trigger that more intercession is needed to see a lasting breakthrough.

The following may also be evidence that a breakthrough has come:

- A peaceful rest comes over your heart, similar to a sigh.
- Tears are likely to stop.
- A bubbly feeling of excitement and joy comes from within.
- The Holy Spirit speaks to you.

Sometime ago, in preparation for a class I was to teach, I was looking for the word "intercession" in the dictionary. But my eyes fell on the words "intercept" and "interchange." It seemed the Holy Spirit spoke to my heart, *Alice, this is how the kingdom of God destroys the kingdom of Satan.*

The word "intercept" is a verb, requiring action. To intercept something you must stop or interrupt its progress or course of action. "Interchange" means to replace one thing with another. "Intercession" is to stand in the gap between what is happening and what God wants to happen. So, the intercessor intercepts the plan of the enemy and causes a spiritual interchange.

David F. Wells, a professor of Historical and Systematic Theology states, "What, then, is the nature of petitionary prayer? It is, in essence, rebellion—rebellion against the world in its fallenness, the absolute and undying refusal to accept as normal what is pervasively abnormal. It is, in this its negative aspect, the refusal of every agenda, every scheme, every interpretation that is at odds with the norm as originally established by God."[6] Intercession is expressing a holy dissatisfaction with the way things are and taking the necessary steps to bring change through prayer.

I envision a day will come when thousands of intercessors with militant, reckless abandonment for Jesus will *stand up* for the lost, *stand against* the powers of darkness and *stand* for the kingdom of God. They will be radical. John the Baptist was radical! Paul was radical! Elijah was radical! Are you radical when it comes to prayer? We need to heed the challenge Dick Eastman gives us in his book *The Jericho Hour*:

> Intercessors who become weary in their warfare would do well to remember that our victory is already assured. We only must fight! Note Paul's concluding promise to Roman believers that "the God of peace will crush Satan under your feet" (Rom. 16:20). The word "crush" is from the Greek *suntribo* meaning "to trample upon, break in pieces, shatter, bruise, grind down and smash." What could be more decisive? Indeed, our victory is decisive in every way. It is assured over the world (1 John 5:4,5), over the flesh (Gal. 5:24; Rom. 7:22-25), over all that exalts itself against God (2 Cor. 10:5) and even over death and the grave (1 Cor. 15:54,55).[7]

"A story is told that in the darkest hour of the war with Germany, when the destiny of civilization was trembling in the balance, the Congress of Allied Women meeting in Paris adopted the ringing slogan, 'Believe victory! Think victory! Preach victory! Live victory!'"[8] The Church of Jesus Christ would do well to make this its slogan in these days of turbulent and fierce spiritual battle.

## AM I MY BROTHER'S KEEPER?

And speaking of spiritual battles, did you know that the Lord will use an intercessor to help save the life of another? In the book of Jonah, God asked Jonah to go to the city of Nineveh to prophesy and call for repentance. Instead, Jonah chose a little "R & R," not rest and relaxation, but rebel and run. Consequently, Jonah found himself spending three days and three nights—not in the plush Hyatt Regency Hotel—but in the belly of a fish! The Lord was insistent that Jonah was His "man for the hour." Jonah repented, and the fish vomited him up on dry land. With holy fear, Jonah obeyed the Lord's call to go into Nineveh. Revival came to Nineveh, but Jonah was angry. With shocking and penetrating clarity Jonah retorted:

> O Lord, is this not what I said when I was still at home? That is why I was so quick to flee to Tarshish. I knew that you are a gracious and compassionate God, slow to anger and abounding in love, a God who relents from sending calamity. Now, O Lord, take away my life, for it is better for me to die than to live (Jon. 4:2,3).

The Lord argued His point for sparing Nineveh after Jonah spewed his complaints. God said:

> But Nineveh has more than a hundred and twenty thousand people who cannot tell their right hand from their left, and many cattle as well. Should I not be concerned about that great city? (v. 11).

If the Lord will go to these lengths to save sinful Nineveh, we should be encouraged that the Lord will also speak to us for the sake of others.

One Monday morning during prayer, I sensed the Holy Spirit speak to me concerning my brother, John Day, a State Farm Insurance agent in Waco, Texas. I received a quick mental picture of John in a car accident, with a distinct feeling that the enemy was planning to kill him. This spiritual news flash wasn't hard to believe, considering "the thief comes only to steal and kill and destroy" (John 10:10). As my husband, Eddie, says, "Sometimes the Lord lets you see the cards the enemy is holding." Immediately, I took this need before the Lord. I prayed:

> Lord, thank You for this assignment. I accept the call to intercede, and I trust that as I pray, You will stop the

enemy's plan for my brother. Thank You for the promises given to me about Your purposes for John's life. I stand with You this day against Satan's plan for my brother.

Then I stopped praying and opened my eyes. (We do not pray to Satan, we speak to him as Jesus did.) I said:

Spirits of darkness, as an ambassador of the Lord Jesus Christ, you are under my authority. Jesus has told me about your evil plot. You have no right to my brother. I bind every effort to kill him in the name of Jesus Christ. I command you to loose him now.

All day the burden to pray would come and go. I continued to offer up my prayers without doubt or unbelief. Tuesday, I called him. "John, how are you doing?" I asked.

He replied, "Praise the Lord, I'm doing just great, Alice Lee. God is good, isn't He? Wow! We serve a great God!"

If you feel you must warn someone of pending danger, please use caution with your words. To have called my brother and said, "John, the Lord showed me a vision of you dying in a car accident," would not have been a blessing! It could have bred fear in his heart.

Job said, "What I feared has come upon me; what I dreaded has happened to me" (Job 3:25).

I did not tell my brother the specifics, but I did ask him to be extra careful while driving during that week. After advising Eddie to pray, I called our friend, Pastor John Foster, to agree with us in prayer for my brother's life. Throughout the week the urgency continued, so I kept praying. During our Sunday evening church service, I slipped out to call my brother. He was in church, so I left the following message on his recorder:

"John, you know the Lord has had several of us pray for you this week. I believe He has revealed the enemy's plan to harm you. Please be very careful. We are continuing to intercede for your safety." (Notice that when I was given permission to share this with him, I worded it carefully so as not to cause fear to come upon him.) I purposely avoided words like "kill" and "car wreck."

At 11:00 P.M. John returned my call. "How did you know that

I might have a car accident?" he asked. "Friday, I almost had a head-on collision. I remembered your caution while I was in my car. It may be strange, but I have had this eerie feeling that the enemy was trying to kill me. Then Saturday, while stopped at a red light, I was hit from behind. I'm okay, though. I'm grateful that the Lord revealed this to you."

Because of the prayer covering, Satan's scheme was defeated. Yes, he was hit from the rear—it's just like the enemy to slip up from the backside!

Why was he even in a wreck after our prayer? God gave us victory! The enemy wanted him dead; God wants him alive! Ours is to obey, not to question. I am convinced John is alive today because of prayer. Can you see how standing in the gap can change the outcome of what would have otherwise happened? There really was an interception of the enemy's plan, and an interchange as a result of intercession.

You might ask, "Does God really put us in that kind of position?"

Yes, He does!

Teaching at a large church in Singapore in January 1994, I was asked, "Are you suggesting that God would put something as serious as life and death in the hands of an intercessor?"

That question sounds strangely like Cain's question, "Am I my brother's keeper?" (Gen. 4:9) Absolutely! And this is war! In war real casualties occur! It is time for the Church to awaken from its slumber and realize the dimensions of its responsibility on earth! After all, intercession is now Jesus' full-time occupation.

The writer of Hebrews reminds us that "Therefore he is able to save completely those who come to God through him, because he always lives to intercede for them" (7:25). At times, the intercessor is to stand in the gap for one's eternal life (his or her salvation). At other times, the intercessor will be called on to stand in the gap for one's physical life and safety, as well.

When we receive a word from God to pray, we should first agree with God and accept the burden. Second, through prayer and faith, we should identify the fact that the Lord wants to change the situation. Third, we should intercept by praying for mercy. Finally, we should pray believing that a transfer has taken place in the heavenlies as God releases His provision.

## INTERCESSION: PERSEVERING PRAYER

We need to pray faithfully until we see a breakthrough. The great intercessor George Müeller said, "When once I am persuaded that a thing is right, I go on praying for it until the end comes. I never give up until the answer comes. The great fault of the children of God is that they do not continue in prayer. They do not persevere. If they desire anything for God's glory, they should pray until they get it."[9]

Continuing in prayer for a need is not unbelief. If the burden is still on your heart, then continue to pray! The Lord will not give you a false burden. The very fact you still sense an urgency for breakthrough is enough to believe the victory is yet to come. The Lord can tell us when a breakthrough occurs. And until He does, we must pray. Jesus taught the importance of praying with persistence.

> Then Jesus told his disciples a parable to show them that they should always pray and not give up. He said: "In a certain town there was a judge who neither feared God nor cared about men. And there was a widow in that town who kept coming to him with the plea, 'Grant me justice against my adversary.' For some time he refused. But finally he said to himself, 'Even though I don't fear God or care about men, yet because this widow keeps bothering me, I will see that she gets justice, so that she won't eventually wear me out with her coming!' And the Lord said, "Listen to what the unjust judge says. And will not God bring about justice for his chosen ones, who cry out to him day and night? Will he keep putting them off?" (Luke 18:1-7).

The Lord is not punitive and mean. He is not sitting on His throne like a pompous King, laughing at us as we pray. Absolutely not! His intention for this kind of persistence is to instill an unwavering faith in the face of every obstacle. And this kind of faith is developed by stretching our faith muscles. The last verse of this parable finishes with, "I tell you, he will see that they get justice, and quickly. However, when the Son of Man comes, will he find faith on the earth?" (v. 8).

Well known theologian Walter Wink has said, "History belongs to the intercessors."[10] I believe the *future* belongs to them as well. We, the Bride of Christ, should find a place in this world where we will invest our prayers, our tears, our fasting and our

........................................................................

*Intercession is a passion,
not a pastime.*

........................................................................

very lives. Many of us are selfishly serving the trinity of the flesh, "me, myself and I." The Lord is looking for those who are willing to extend the kingdom of God into the Church, the city, the nation and the world through prayer. Intercession is a *passion*, not a *pastime*.

Perhaps you are wondering, *How do I get that calling?*

The answer is found in Matthew 25:23:

His master replied, "Well done, good and faithful servant! You have been faithful with a few things; I will put you in charge of many things. Come and share your master's happiness!"

## BE FAITHFUL IN SMALL THINGS

Ashlee is our youngest daughter. When she was almost six years old, she and a young friend were trying to choose which Saturday morning cartoon to watch. After some searching, Ashlee came into the den where Eddie was studying.

She asked, "Daddy, can I watch *Ghost Busters*?"

Eddie replied, "No, Ashlee, I think you can find something better to watch."

Ashlee conceded with a smile and left to look for something else. Soon she returned to ask about another program. Eddie again suggested she look for something better to watch. The third time she approached him, Eddie pointed to her chest and asked,

"Ashlee, who lives in here?"

She looked down at her chest and answered, "Jesus."

Gently he counseled, "Ashlee, Jesus lives in you. You can watch any program He says you can watch."

With a smile and a sense of relief, Ashlee turned to leave. Suddenly she stopped to explain, "Dad, the reason I was asking you is just in case I don't get in touch with Him today." The truth is, we all have days when we don't get in touch with Him.

Ashlee was trying to be faithful over the small things in her life!

Because of Ashlee's faithfulness over small things, in May of 1995, at age 11, Ashlee was one of the 50 children participating in the Global Consultation on World Evangelism held in Seoul, Korea. Children can be dynamic prayer warriors. God used these children in Korea to light a passion in the hearts of the other 4,000 church delegates from around the world.

It all begins with being faithful over the little things in our lives!

If you want God to give you a vision for Israel, or a burden for your city or the world, then be faithful to intercede for your family, neighbors, pastors and church. Be faithful in prayer over a few things and He will enlarge the horizons of your spiritual authority! We cannot expect to be given the kind of revelation Moses received if we are not first faithful to walk in obedience like Joshua. As we obey step by step, the Father can trust us with greater spiritual authority. We must be faithful over those things we can see before we can expect to be trusted with the unseen.

Intercession calls for us to deal with the unseen. John Piper was quoted by David Bryant, in his article, "Reflections on Spiritual Warfare and the Ministry of United Prayer":

> If you do not know that life is war, you will not know what prayer is for. In the Christian life, life is war, a spiritual battle that happens to us from the day we are born to the day we die.[11]

This personal spiritual struggle is part of the larger, unseen conflict that is being played out in the heavenlies. The outcome of the battle is already decided. All who have placed their faith in Christ will eventually participate in its victory. However, the intercessor is involved in enforcing the defeat of the enemy. Are you ready? You *can* intercept the enemy's progress and bring about a spiritual interchange.

Let me encourage you to move beyond the veil, touch the heart of God and regard the "triggers" of your own heart as you partner with Him in defeating the enemy!

## UNVEILING THE TRUTH ABOUT YOU

1. What are some indications that God is training you to be an intercessor? Are you willing to learn? What are the fears you have about this calling?
2. What are the ways God speaks to you? Are you able to accept the reality that what you think you heard is not what He said? Do you fear misunderstanding Him?
3. Are you a trustworthy person? Can you hold revelation you have received from God until He releases you to share it? Is *information* or *intimacy* more important to you during prayer? Why?
4. What are some physical "triggers" God has used in your life? Did you understand what you were to do at the time you received them?

**Notes**
1. C. Peter Wagner, *Prayer Shield* (Ventura, Calif.: Regal Books, 1992), pp. 26-27.
2. John and Paula Sandford, *Elijah Task* (Tulsa, Okla.: Victory House, Inc., 1977), p. 106.
3. Cindy Jacobs, *The Voice of God* (Ventura, Calif.: Regal Books, 1995), p. 102.
4. Cindy Jacobs, *Possessing the Gates of the Enemy* (Tarrytown, N.Y.: Chosen Books, 1991), p. 63.
5. C. Peter Wagner, *Prayer Shield* (Ventura, Calif.: Regal Books, 1992), p. 27.
6. David F. Wells, *Perspectives on the World Christian Movement* (Pasadena, Calif.: William Carey Library, 1981), p. 124.
7. Dick Eastman, *The Jericho Hour* (Orlando, Fla.: Creation House, 1994), p. 100.
8. Reverend G.B.F. Hallock, *Best Modern Illustrations* (New York: Harper & Brothers Publishers, 1935), p. 371.
9. George Müeller, "How to Get Your Prayers Answered," *Sounds of the Trumpet*, 1985, p. 29.
10. Walter Wink, "Prayer and the Powers," *Sojourners*, (October 1990): p. 10.
11. John Quam, "Reflections on Spiritual Warfare and the Ministry of United Prayer," Introduction for David Bryant. Article where John Quam quotes John Piper.

# CHAPTER THREE

# Cultivating a Lifestyle of Intercession

## ON-THE-JOB TRAINING

The *role* of intercession is the duty of every Christian, however many Christians are unaware of the difference between the *role* and the *gift* of intercession. Peter Wagner provides insight about this difference in his book *Prayer Shield*:

> All Christians, without exception, have roles that parallel most of the gifts. For example, not all Christians have the gift of an evangelist, but all have the role of being witnesses for Christ and leading people to the Lord.[1]

Jesus did not say, "If you pray," but "When you pray." It is important for every believer to pray. Therefore, we can conclude that all Christians are given the role of "intercession." And yet not everyone who prays has the *gift* of intercession.

## MANY ROLES, DIFFERENT CALLINGS

I define the gift of intercession as "a special grace given by Christ to pray for extended lengths of time on the basis of an intimate relationship."

This gift does not make intercessors more special to God than others, just more available for prayer. Surveys have shown that the average American pastor spends 15 to 22 minutes a day in prayer, and the average American Christian prays less than that. But intercessors, as a rule, spend much more time in the prayer closet and sense real joy and fulfillment in doing so. As with all spiritual gifts, people spend time doing what their gifts motivate them to do.

And because intercessors are motivated to pray, hours in prayer seem like minutes to them. They are drawn into timelessness as they enter the realm of the Spirit to worship the Lord wholeheartedly. These times are used by the Holy Spirit to move them from one spiritual level to another. Their hunger for more of God drives them to make time for intimacy with Him. Prayer is not usually an effort for intercessors.

Of course, seasons in life do occur when such desires are difficult to fulfill, such as in the case of a young mother with babies,

*Prayer is a relationship, not a ritual.*

a busy executive or a single parent, etc. And when these seasons arrive, intercessors must be creative in preparing times and places for prayer.

Times and places for prayer are as diverse as the people who pray. As I mentioned earlier, we are all called to the role of intercession, therefore those of us who do not have the gift of intercession are required to employ discipline and obedience with regard to prayer.

Yonggi Cho, pastor of the world's largest church in Seoul, Korea, says he spends 1 to 3 hours in prayer each day. Some believers strive to tithe their time; some pray 2.4 hours a day (calculated on a 24-hour day). Others pray a tithe of their waking time, or 1.6 hours each day. Start with small amounts of time talking with Jesus. As you get to know Him, you will want to be with Him more and more.

Whatever time you give to the Lord in prayer will bless Him and you. Remember, prayer is a relationship, not a ritual. And the more time you invest in a relationship, the more intimacy and trust you will develop. Whether you have the role of intercession or the gift of intercession, spending time with Christ is key to your Christian walk.

## PROPHESYING THE BURDEN

Although intercession is not listed as "a gift" in Ephesians 4, 1 Corinthians 12 or Romans 12, the gift of prophecy is occasionally interchanged with intercession. For example, the Hebrew word *massa* is translated "to prophesy a burden or to declare an utterance."

Often in the Old Testament the prophets uttered the burden of the Lord. (See Jer. 23:33-40; Ezek. 12:10; Dan. 9:20-23.) The gift of intercession can be expressed through prayer in a variety of ways. (See 2 Sam. 12:16,17; 2 Chron. 15:14,15; Zech. 12:10,11.) For example, the Hebrew word *paga*, "intercession" means "to prophesy, or invade by violence, to struggle in prayer, or contend with an adversary, to fight or labor fervently, with force, crowd and press forward, or seize, to catch, travail and weep, to come between."

I believe that not only is there the *role* and the *gift* of intercession, but there is also an *office* of intercession. This office is recognized when the gifts of intercession and administration are coupled to create a leadership role in the Body. The Church should release into ministry those with the office of intercession and acknowledge that God has set them apart to help equip the Body of Christ for intercession. A person called to the *office* of intercession can often impart a passion for intercession.

Not only do those called to the office of intercession carry "spiritual weight" before the throne of God, but they can also inspire others with similar gifts and callings.

The role, the gift and the office are true and necessary intercessory callings in the Body of Christ. Together they work to accomplish the Lord's purpose. And to accomplish His purpose in the Body, the different callings and levels of intercessors require that we each identify our own callings. As 1 Corinthians

12 teaches, one person functions as an eye, one as a foot and still another as an ear. Although each part of the Body functions in a different gift, they unite in their service to Christ.

## INTERCESSION: ONE MINISTRY—MANY GIFTS

Our unity in service is best seen in our diversity of gifts. And each person's gift mix is unlike any other person's. The place each of us is called to fill in the Body can be filled by no one else. Therefore, if we pattern our intercession after another (emulation), we will be frustrated, ineffective and confused. To emulate another is a work of the flesh (see Gal. 5:20). We are to be imitators of Christ and not the flesh in each other.

According to 1 Corinthians 12, "There are different kinds of gifts" (v. 4); "different kinds of service" (v. 5); and "different kinds of working" (v. 6). All the gifts work together for the same God. Consequently, Christians with the gift of intercession will have different ministries working through them, because other gifts such as mercy or teaching or word of knowledge will affect the way they pray.

By looking at the diversity in our gifts, we can see the need for the different kinds of intercessors required to create a whole ministry of intercession. Let's consider just a few:

### Administrative Intercessors
The "administrative intercessors" have the gifts of leadership, giving, exhortation, faith and administration. They serve as the "spinal cord" in the Body carrying orders to other members. They coordinate and form prayer chains, telephone networks, newsletters and crisis lines so everyone will be notified and encouraged to pray. Without these administrators, much of the intercession we experience today would lack the order and follow through these steadfast men and women of God provide.

### Cafeteria-Style Intercessors
These are men and women who intercede "cafeteria style." Their prayer lives are continually changing. Like chameleons, they do not conform to any particular mode or method. They are pliable

and flexible in the hand of God. They can discern the Spirit's direction, whether in travail, warfare or prayer lists. These intercessors easily enter the flow of the Spirit. Even new believers can intercede effectively in this way.

## Crisis Intercessors

These intercessors pray for emergencies and can recognize when traumatic events have occurred. Like an E.M.S. ambulance driver, this "emergency intercessor" is always on call. Emergency intercessors sense the urgency in every crisis. They are the search and rescue team for those who are wounded on the spiritual battlefield. Their gifts might include: prophecy, mercy, faith, healing, pastor and service. We must have these intense people who receive emergency calls and send immediate intercessory help.

## Intercessors for the Nations

Today, God is calling more intercessors for the nations than has ever been recorded by the Church. These are the evangelists in the Body of Christ. They may have a gift mix of evangelism, prophecy, faith and mercy. These intercessors stand in the gap for different nations of the world to pray in the last great revival before Christ's return.

## Mercy-Motivated Intercessors

From a merciful "heart" mercy-motivated intercessors find great satisfaction praying for any event, city, nation or situation needing the mercy of the Lord. They breathe compassion and empathy into the spiritual lives of others and are able to touch the heartache of another with encouragement and love. Mercy-motivated intercessors often move in the gifts of counseling, healing, giving and helps.

## Prayer-Evangelism Intercessors

These intercessors pray toward evangelism, ministry and service to others. They act as the "knees" of the Body. They can cross the street or the city on their knees with prayer for the lost. Their prayers often result in sending workers to the right people in the right place for the right reason—bringing others to Christ. Their gifts often include faith, service and evangelism.

## Prayer-List Intercessors

Some intercessors pray through prayer lists. They tend to have the gift of administration or teacher mentioned in Romans 12. These "prayer-list intercessors" tend to be disciplined as they faithfully pray through the assignments God gives them on their ordered prayer lists. Occasionally they will get emergency requests and prophetic instruction, but their priority is to be persevering for the people, places and issues on their prayer lists.

## Prophetic Intercessors

There are "prophetic intercessors" who seem to hear from God almost as much as they speak to God. Exhortation, faith, wisdom, words of knowledge and discernment flow from the prophetic intercessor. Paul mentioned the eyes and ears of the Body in 1 Corinthians 12. He points out that if the whole body were an eye, there would be no hearing. With those who are "eyes" and "ears" (prophetic intercessors), God often shares the secrets of His heart and the strategies of His work. God reveals His plans to them. At times He reveals the plans of the enemy, as well.

## Special Assignment Intercessors

Other intercessors have a special assignment to pray for leaders, such as religious, political or social leaders. They have a nurturing pastoral gift. They love to minister and shepherd in prayer, and quite often intercede with great compassion. The primary concern of the "special assignment intercessor" is the protection and care given the Body of Christ. They also feel deeply about the leaders for whom they pray. At times they become emotionally attached to them. Leadership can misunderstand them if they do not appreciate the shepherding heart of these prayer intercessors.

## Warfare Intercessors

Some intercessors are prayer warriors involved in spiritual warfare, which requires the revelatory gifts spoken of in 1 Corinthians 12. These gifts might include: faith, word of knowledge, discernment of spirits or prophecy. Prayer warriors are aware of the battle in the heavenlies (see Eph. 6:12). If the Body of Christ does not understand and learn from these intercessors, they will not see the spiritual battle developing. Like a spiritual radar installation, a prayer warrior is constantly surveying the heavenlies. When he or she locks in on a prayer concern, this warrior has a gift to be "an eye" in the Body of Christ. The Lord reveals enemy targets that need to be demolished. Like the "smart bombs" of Desert Storm, this kind of intercession is activated by the Spirit of God to hit a specific target.

## CORPORATE INTERCESSION

All the gifts should work together for the good of the Body. And yet, several reasons can be cited for the ineffectiveness of corporate prayer. One reason is that we sometimes expect everyone to pray like ourselves, as though we all have the same spiritual gift. When someone does not conform to our criteria for intercession, we can easily grieve the Holy Spirit by rejecting that person's method of communing with God.

Another reason corporate prayer becomes ineffective is that we fail to recognize that we are all at different levels of spiritual maturity. This is not bad, it is just a fact. However, when someone imitates the anointing of another, not only does the entire group suffer, but the Holy Spirit is also grieved. We are cautioned in Romans 12:3, "Do not think of yourself more highly than you ought, but rather think of yourself with sober judgment, in accordance with the measure of faith God has given you."

## HOLY CHAOS

Unmet expectations and failure to recognize the uniqueness of others within the corporate Body can produce holy chaos. For example: The prayer meeting begins. One brother is mercy motivated. He prays with passion and tears, as a fevered crisis erupts in his heart. His unbridled emotion irritates the woman next to him. Her primary gift is administration, so in her mind she is saying, *If they would just let me organize this group, we could really accomplish something.*

Across the room is an intercessor who discerns a spiritual battle raging. Because of a strong gift of discernment, this believer reacts with warfare prayer. With predictable intensity, she thrashes her hands through the air, screaming fiercely at the rulers of darkness. Others sitting in the room are thinking, *My God, someone give this poor woman a Prozac to calm her down!*

Following her is a man who always prays from prayer lists— for him it's almost a sin to do otherwise! As he prays in his calculating manner, others are grieving God by saying, "This is a waste of time."

Next, comes the seasoned prayer warrior who completely intimidates the rest of the group by praying refined and polished prayers.

Eventually that one who is totally "off-track" begins to pray. When the group is directed to pray for reconciliation regarding racial division, this person shifts gears and begins to pray for the puppy caught in the drain pipe. There is no focus, no flow. The result is a mess! What is the answer?

All of us have been in these kinds of prayer meetings. Frankly, we must come to appreciate our diversity in unity. Corporate intercession can be effective, and as powerful as a nuclear warhead if each member will accept the others' spiritual gifts. Remember, all gifts must be governed by love. As we come to understand teamwork and cooperation, our different ways of praying will work like a well-oiled machine. I do not pray like others; I do not expect others to pray like me. The discipline of God in each life will affect that person's depth of prayer. If we accept each individual's style of prayer, understanding he or she prays from his or her motivational gift, then God will be blessed, the enemy crippled and the group united.

Do we believe it is wrong to use prayer lists? Is warfare prayer wrong? Should we hold back our tears? No. Each of these facets of intercession is appropriate because they *work together* toward the common end.

## SPIRIT-LED SPIRITUAL LEADERSHIP

For effective corporate intercession to occur, the leader must begin with clear instruction. The leader's job is to discern the Holy Spirit's direction and to point the way for the prayers of those in attendance. We are facilitators in the Body to help each pray from his or her Spirit-led gift. This is accomplished as the leader does the following:

1. The leader begins by inviting the Holy Spirit to reveal the Father's assignment for those in attendance to pray. This corporate time is NOT ABOUT PERSONAL ISSUES! It is a time to hear the burden of the Lord together and ascend, as one Body, into the heavenlies through intercession. Powerful intercession can flow without disturbing the individuality of each one who prays.
2. The leader is responsible for giving firm, loving direction during the corporate prayer time, which may include:
   - Gently interrupting a person who has a misdirected prayer (off-track) by asking him or her to return to a particular issue;
   - Stopping a person who continues to monopolize the prayer time. If this becomes a problem, either approach the person in love and whisper, "Please don't pray again this evening so others have the opportunity to participate" or say aloud, "Would you please also allow others the privilege of praying?"
   - Preventing a person from gossiping in their prayers about private matters that should not be publicly known. You may have to intervene by saying something such as, "These are not issues that all of us need to know about. I would prefer moving on to something else."
   - Halting a person's condemning and judgmental prayers by reminding the group that God alone is the Judge and that our responsibility is to ask the Lord for mercy in all situations.

      The leader, however, must discern when the team has drifted from the Holy Spirit's direction and should not be afraid to lead for the benefit of staying on track. Begin by admitting that as a leader you may blow it, but let people know that direction is essential for the group prayer time. Often I have messed up, but the group is supportive because I remain teachable and humble.

3. While each intercessor will petition the Lord in different ways, the leader helps maintain unity of heart. The
   guideline for corporate intercession is to maintain the
   same train of thought throughout the prayer time. For
   instance: Start with Bosnia, then move to political
   unrest in Bosnia, next the children in Bosnia and on to
   salvation for the people of Bosnia. Most groups become
   distracted when they change tracks. They might start
   with the political unrest in Bosnia, then someone
   moves to praying about abortion in India and another
   prays for the Sunday morning worship service. Can
   you see the splintering? So, the leader's responsibility
   is to attempt to maintain a unity of thought among the
   group.

Unity may be seen as silence blankets the room. A holy hush
suggests that each heart is discerning the will of the Father for the
hour. Then without warning, a woman passionately asks the
Lord to forgive them as a church for alienating the African-
Americans who live in the neighborhood. She weeps with agony
that soon involves the others.

A man with the burden of evangelism earnestly asks the
Lord for the salvation of the African-Americans in the city and
petitions the Lord to open doors. Immediately, a man fervently
repents for offending his neighbor who is black and promises the
Lord to make it right. The Holy Spirit gently prompts a gifted
teacher to read a portion of Scripture about unity and the
prophetically-gifted person speaks an encouraging word.

A few moments later another person cries out for racial reconciliation and healing in the nation. Fully absorbed in the unity
of prayer, the faith to believe God soars. The cycle of intercession
flows steadily with prayer focused on reconciliation. Then like a
weight lifted, the group explodes in spontaneous clapping. Quiet
settles over the group again, as every believer senses the presence
of God. United, corporate intercession has occurred. At the end
of the prayer time, the leader should spend a few minutes
debriefing the group concerning what God was saying to them
individually and corporately. This time of recapping brings a
sense of purpose, balance and unity.

## THE BALANCED BODY

As we have discovered, the ministry of intercession requires many gifts within the Body. All these gifts working and praying together keep the Body healthy. But it is the gift of discernment mentioned in 1 Corinthians 12 that helps the Body to maintain a balance and accountability for what it receives. Because of this need to discern, the Lord will often give dreams and physical symptoms to intercessors as burdens in the body for warnings to intercede. These warnings help the intercessor to identify what is happening in the lives of others. But if the intercessor fails to realize that the physical symptoms come as indicators from the Lord for prayer and fails to detach himself or herself from these burdens, the intercessor might become psychotic and paranoid.

Years of counseling others have convinced me that many intercessors silently suffer in hospitals and mental institutions because they have misunderstood the burdens of God. In our secular society we look for medical relief for our burdens, when the need is often for "prayer relief."

In making this statement, I do not intend to negate every case where legitimate chemical imbalances might exist, however, much more attention needs to be given to spiritual causes in psychological and even biological problems.

Some intercessors have been accused of having psychosomatic health problems. The word "psychosomatic" comes from two Greek words. The first is *psyche*, meaning "soul"—the mind, will and emotions or response center of a person. The second word is *soma*, meaning "body." Thus it is possible to have psychosomatic symptoms from ignoring and refusing to respond to the physical burdens representing the need to pray.

## BURDEN BEARING TRAITS

Throughout the years, I have noticed that those who are called to a life of intercession have certain characteristics—both good and not-so-good traits. Let's look at a few.

In one sense, an intercessor is a "burden bearer." Being a bur-

den bearer can be difficult and requires faithfulness. Our faithfulness is first to the Father and His purposes. We are to love the
Father and receive His love. When our hearts are knit to His, our
love will be reflected in our responses—as was the case in the following story:

> A kind old woman, passing down the street, saw a little
> girl carrying a heavy baby boy who was almost as large
> as herself. "Isn't that a heavy load you're carrying, little
> girl?" asked the woman.
> "No ma'am," the little girl flashed back, "he's my
> brother."[2]

But as I briefly mentioned in chapter 2, you may misunderstand the heaviness or sense of depression (burden bearing) that
comes upon you for no apparent reason. You and your family are
well, yet your emotions are suddenly unsettled. You may feel
sad; you may even find yourself on the verge of tears. Thinking
that this is wrong, you might seek counsel. Some seek medica-
tion, while others assume some hidden sin needs to be uncov-
ered in their lives, even though the Lord brings nothing to mind.

Rarely does it dawn on us that this unsettling may be the
burden of the Lord. The heaviness may not be related to you per-
sonally at all! It may have been placed there by the Lord to "trigger" you to intercede. God may be calling you to the prayer closet without telling you specifically why. At these times, you must
agree with God and trust Him with the details.

Sometimes God will begin to bring illumination as you pray.
Years passed before I finally began to recognize and understand
the ways of God. The Lord has to break through the spiritual
dimension and into our physical realm to trigger the mind to
pray. My interviews with many intercessors have revealed that it
is not uncommon for an intercessor to experience a dull ache in
the heart. This pain may be a physical symptom of the Lord's
pain for those in need.

When you don't know what to pray for, "go fishing." I will
usually begin by praying for family members. I troll through my
list of names. Nothing. Then "I cast the line out" into the community and then the city and then the nation. Possibly a trau-

matic event is God's assignment. Suddenly there's a tug on the line, which tells me I have "a bite" and the struggle begins! A passion to pray heightens and I hang on until I have experienced a sense of release.

Realize that at times the Lord reserves the details for Himself. I find that this is one of the most difficult times of intercession. It requires inordinate faith to pray, without knowledge, until the release comes.

Why are more women than men called into the ministry of intercession? Peter Wagner suggests, in his book *Prayer Shield*, that the answer could be related to their experience of giving birth. He writes, "Mothers know even better than could the apostle Paul the full meaning of his statement, 'My little children, for whom I labor in birth again until Christ is formed in you'" (Gal. 4:19, *NKJV*).[3] Yet, I am encouraged to say that in the last 12 months, it has been my experience to see more men accept the call of intercession than in the previous decades.

## BIRTHING ANSWERS THROUGH DEATH TO SELF

Intercessors are acquainted with travail, and as Paul says, they are acquainted with death. Jesus taught, "Greater love has no one than this, that he lay down his life for his friends" (John 15:13).

In his book *The Ministry of Intercession*, Andrew Murray says, "Prayer is a form of crucifixion, of our fellowship with Christ's cross, of our giving up our flesh to the death."[4]

No self-interests are allowed beyond the veil in God's Holy of Holies. Death to self is a vital part of experiencing the fullness of Christ (see Gal. 2:20). As we abandon our goals, careers, future successes and desires, the crucifixion of self becomes complete. In Rees Howell's biography, *Intercessor*, we read:

> But before He can lead a chosen vessel into such a life of intercession, He first has to deal to the bottom with all that is natural. Love of money, personal ambition, natural affection for parents and loved ones, the appetites of the body, the love of life itself, all that makes even a con-

verted man live unto himself, for his own comfort or advantage, for his own advancement, even for his own circle of friends, has to go to the cross. It is no theoretical death, but a real crucifixion with Christ, such as only the Holy Ghost Himself can make actual in the experience of His servant. Both as a crisis and process, Paul's testimony must be made ours: "I have been and still am crucified with Christ." The self must be released from itself to become the agent of the Holy Ghost.[5]

Faithfulness to the Father involves both loving Him and knowing Him. Paul emphasizes the importance of knowing the ways of God. "I want to know Christ and the power of his resurrection and the fellowship of sharing in his sufferings, becoming like him in his death" (Phil. 3:10). Loving Jesus like the Father loves Him is crucial

........................................................

*The Father has no favorites, but He does have intimates.*

........................................................

in developing intimacy. Jesus is not a principle, nor is He a "cliché" used in spiritual warfare. He is a person to be passionately pursued. And this is how we cultivate intimacy with Him.

I see a dangerous trend today. Some intercessors are becoming infatuated with the enemy and committed to warfare without having developed a deep level of intimacy with God. This is a subtle but serious danger. Undoubtedly we have an enemy to war against for the souls of humanity. However, do not forget to first "draw near to God" (intimacy); then "resist the Devil" (warfare).

## NO FAVORITES, ONLY INTIMATES

The Father has no favorites, but He does have intimates. The

Body of Christ today is beginning to desire Him. And the Father wants intimacy with us more than we want intimacy with Him. Unbelievably, God is looking for homemakers, lawyers, plumbers, surveyors, teachers and people from all walks of life who will fellowship with Him! He can only share His heart with those who delight to be in His presence in the prayer closet.

Many of us want to know the secrets of the Father's heart. We want His anointing upon our lives. But we are unwilling to make the necessary investment before His throne.

As Mike Bickle, senior pastor of Metro Vineyard Fellowship in Kansas City, has said, "We will not be able to impart what we do not possess. We can repeat doctrines at an intellectual level without imparting life. We each play an important role in determining the degree of intimacy we have with the Lord. If we're content with a small measure of intimacy, then that's all we will experience. If we are willing to pay a price for deeper intimacy, we will experience it."[6]

The ultimate Christian experience is intimate union with God. Not only does intimacy satisfy our need for relationship, but it also compels us to intercede in order that His Kingdom be established on earth.

To whom do you tell your secrets? Probably someone who is trustworthy; someone who cares; someone with whom you have fellowship; someone who understands and identifies with you. This is the kind of person the Father is seeking. He will share the secrets of His heart with those He trusts—those who will not share His secrets with another until the appointed time. The Bible says, "A gossip betrays a confidence, but a trustworthy man [or woman] keeps a secret" (Prov. 11:13). The trustworthy person will not gloat over the revelation of heavenly mysteries, as Paul refused to do in 2 Corinthians 12.

An intimate intercessor should spend much time listening. Normally, prayer is a two-way conversation, but sometimes we are just to listen, as was the experience recorded by Daniel in the Scriptures. "Then I heard him speaking, and as I listened to him, I fell into a deep sleep, my face to the ground" (10:9). Silence before God is a key to our relationship with Him. In this sense, silence is truly golden!

A room of quiet...a temple of peace;
The home of faith...where doubtings cease;
A house of comfort...where hope is given;
A source of strength...to make earth heaven;
A shrine of worship...a place to pray
I found all this...in my heart today.[7]

Part of our silence should be spent in *meditation*. To meditate, as it is generally understood, means "to ponder, contemplate, or become absorbed in thought." This is a discipline that requires time and practice. Like a master pickpocket, however, Satan seeks to sabotage our time and snatch God's truth from our minds.

Successful meditation includes three building blocks:

**Building Block 1: Isolation**
Time alone with God is necessary to renew the mind. Romans 12:2 exhorts us to "be transformed by the renewing of your mind. Then you will be able to test and approve what God's will is—his good, pleasing and perfect will."

**Building Block 2: Concentration**
Psalm 1:2 tells us that with concentrative effort we are to "delight [think]...in the law of the Lord, and on his law he meditates day and night."

Isaiah 26:3 instructs us to calm our minds. "You will keep in perfect peace him whose mind is steadfast, because he trusts in you." The flesh or soul—where the mind, will and emotions live—fights against the Spirit, so we must teach it to be in subjection to the Word of God.

**Building Block 3: Association**
We can associate physical objects with spiritual realities. Philippians 4:8 says, "Finally, brothers, whatever is true, whatever is noble, whatever is right, whatever is pure, whatever is lovely, whatever is admirable—if anything is excellent or praiseworthy—think about such things." This verse says to *meditate* on these truths. We do this by storing God's Word in our hearts because His Word is truth (see John 17:17).

If you have a problem with speaking the truth, meditate on

every word coming out of your mouth being true. The Bible declares, "For as he thinketh in his heart, so is he" (Prov. 23:7, KJV). This is not New Age, this is God's Word.

Learn to sit silently and allow the Word to feed your spirit. C. H. Spurgeon said that meditation for a believer is like a cow "chewing her cud." Meditation gets the sweetness and nutrients of God's Word into our hearts and lives. Proper nourishment in the Word produces fruit. By meditating we digest the Word so spiritual growth and effectiveness can occur.

It is impossible to separate God from His Word. Therefore, the more time we spend in His Word, the more we will become like Him. And as we grow in His likeness, our lives will become "others centered."

## INTERCESSORS: PEOPLE WHO CARE ABOUT PEOPLE

Intercessors tend to be lovers of people. They want to know people and be involved with them. Not only are they genuinely interested in people, but they are also commonly gifted with "discerning of spirits"—a gift that often allows them to see the hidden intentions of others. God's purpose in providing this gift is not that they "pry," but that they may "pray." When these insights are incorrectly used, intercessors can become judgmental, nosy, suspicious and controlling.

When used properly the gift of discerning of spirits can bring spiritual revelation and power to our prayers. Eddie and I discovered this when we traveled the United States during the 1970s and 1980s as evangelists. By invitation of the pastor, we would travel to a church and hold nightly meetings, lasting as long as two weeks. Sometimes we were the singers; other times Eddie preached.

On one occasion in the early '70s, Eddie and I arrived in a church parking lot with our 24-foot motor home, pulling an 18-foot travel trailer. We were the guest singers for the week. During the staff's lunch break, Eddie returned to the motor home with a church photo directory in his hand.

While he lay down to wait for the pastor to return, I began to look through the photo directory. As my eyes moved from family to family, from individual to individual, I began to pray for them. Though I had never met these people, I sensed the Holy Spirit revealing things to me about them. I circled faces and made margin notes such as, "needs healing; lost; needs the filling of the Holy Spirit; has suffered severe rejection; walking in darkness; etc."

I received this information from the Holy Spirit for the purposes of prayer. On this occasion I was right, but many times I would risk and be wrong. We cannot learn unless we risk, and we do not risk until we try. Failure at this point is not bad—in reality it is part of the death to pride.

Later, Eddie showed my annotated copy of the church directory to the pastor. As he read the notes from page to page, Eddie said that the pastor's eyes began to swell with tears. Soon the pastor was weeping over his flock. He placed the book on the desk and said, "She is exactly right. These are the needs of my people."

Intercessors are usually committed people. They are reliable. They are often doggedly determined about the things of God. I cannot recount to you the scores of times God has revealed to me the need for salvation in the lives of friends. He has led me to pray many hours for them. Because of this intense commitment, I am nicknamed "The Bulldog" among our friends.

Andrew Murray was an intercessor who understood commitment. He writes in *The Ministry of Intercession*:

> There are various elements of importunity. The most important are perseverance, determination, and intensity. Beginning with the refusal to at once accept a denial, importunity grows to the determination to persevere, to spare no time or trouble, until an answer comes. It then rises to the intensity in which the whole being is given to God in supplication, and the boldness comes to grasp God's strength. It can be quiet and restful at times, and passionate and bold at others. It can take time and be patient, and then claim at once what it wants. No matter what its form, it always means and knows that God hears prayer and it will be heard.[8]

Intercessors are committed to God and to others and have genuine desires to see needs met. Eddie and I have nearly 60 personal intercessors who are faithful in their commitment to intercede for us. We cannot begin to tell you how special they are to us! Only the Lord could ever repay them for the investments they make in the Kingdom for us.

## INTERCESSORS ARE PEOPLE, TOO!

I love intercessors! I am one! Writing about their good traits is enjoyable! However, intercessors are people, too, and they can possess some poor human traits. Even the good traits previously mentioned can become fleshy and bad when taken to an extreme. Because of the spiritual burdens they bear, intercessors can easily become moody. Heaviness or depression can creep into the intercessor's life, so we must ask the Holy Spirit whether a burden is genuine or an attack from the enemy. When I'm not sure, I head for the prayer closet, regardless!

Sensitivity to the Holy Spirit is a sought-after trait in an intercessor, however, at times it can preclude our sensitivity to the rest of the Body of Christ. Loud weeping that looks and sounds like a woman in travail may characterize the intercessor's prayer life, but this travailing can be difficult for others to bear. If others are not sensing the same intensity of travail, we should find a private place to pray so we will not confuse or disturb those who may not understand our gifts. The one exception would be when brokenness begins to occur corporately.

Other potential problems can include an intercessor who becomes prideful of his or her relationship with the Lord, expecting others to be like him or her, or when an intercessor tries to dominate a prayer meeting. A wise leader will protect the prayer meeting from monopolizers and manipulators!

Christian leaders are learning about the nature and calling of intercession. As pastoral leadership becomes more aware of the ministry of intercession, their interest in developing intercessors and appropriating the intercessory gifts in the Church will encourage the rest of the Body to pray. Pastors and other spiritual leaders are reading books that explain this unique, hidden and often difficult ministry. They are learning to identify the intercessors in their churches and organizations, making room for this vital ministry. Leadership needs the strength that comes through the ministry of intercession.

Other professions are also beginning to recognize the need for prayer. A Christian psychologist phoned my husband, Eddie, one day to explain, "One of my patients came to you for counseling and seems to have misunderstood what you told her. I am calling to clarify it. My patient understood you to say she is *not* manic depressive and hallucinogenic."

"That is what I said," Eddie replied.

"How can you say that?" asked the doctor.

"First," Eddie questioned, "who said she is those things?"

"That is my diagnosis of her," the doctor replied.

Eddie asked, "Would you like to hear my diagnosis?" With the doctor's permission Eddie continued, "I found her to be more than a conqueror, a joint heir with Jesus, a new creation in Christ, a possessor of all things that pertain to life and godliness...would you like to hear more?"

When the doctor assured Eddie that he had heard enough, Eddie asked, "Do you want her to live up to your diagnosis or mine?"

"Well, yours, of course," the doctor replied.

"Then I think I'd stop giving her yours, Doctor," retorted Eddie. "When she got to my office she was living up to yours!"

"Well, she is clearly hallucinogenic," the doctor insisted.

"Why do you say that?" Eddie asked.

The doctor responded, "She sees things that are not there."

"No," Eddie explained, "She sees things that ARE there."

"You mean..." the doctor paused.

"Yes," Eddie answered.

The doctor then asked if he could come in and discuss these issues. Since then, this psychologist has begun to minister in the power of the Spirit.

Throughout her entire adult life, this lady had experienced depression and anxiety. She had also seen spiritual realities (demons and angels). While praying with her, the Lord revealed to Eddie that this woman was an intercessor. She had never understood the burden of God and how to release it in prayer. As a result, she had failed to realize that her concerns were the Father's concerns. She did not know that her spiritual sight was actually a gift from the Lord that would equip her to engage in spiritual battle in the prayer closet. She was liberated to learn that this was not a curse, but a calling! Well intentioned counselors had told her that prayer burdens were problems. She had been medicated to deal with the burdens that God Himself was placing upon her heart. All she really needed was biblical instruction and encouragement to help her understand the ministry to which God was calling her!

## IT TAKES TIME!

Information will NOT transform you. Formulas will NOT bring you into intimacy with God. A lifestyle of intercession must be cultivated and maintained. Your inner man is like a garden and the disciplines of prayer keep it fertilized, watered, pruned and fruitful. Just as with any garden, time is needed for growth to appear. Seasons of difficulty and sunshine will be part of its life-long development. But these seasons will force the roots deeper into the source of your strength—Jesus Christ. The following illustrates this principle:

> A student asked the president of a school if he could take a shorter course than the one prescribed. "Oh yes," replied the president. "But then it depends upon what you want to be. When God wants to make an oak, He takes a hundred years. When He wants to make a squash, He takes only four months."

God wants you to be an oak tree, not a spiritual squash. To become an oak, your roots must sink down deep. If you are only willing to be a squash, your root system will remain shallow, and you will not have the vitality to linger very long in the Holy of Holies with God.

> Stir me, oh! Stir me, Lord, I care not how,
> But stir my heart in passion for the world!
> Stir me to give, to go—but most of all to pray:
> Stir me, till the blood-red banner be unfurled

Over lands that still in deepest darkness lie,
Or deserts where no cross is lifted high.
Stir me, oh! Stir me, Lord.
Thy heart was stirred by love's intense fire,
Till Thou didst give Thine only Son,
Thy best beloved One,
Even to the dreadful cross, that I might live;
Stir me to give myself so back to Thee
That Thou can give Thyself again through me.
—Author Unknown[9]

Love is the basis for intimacy, and intimacy is the foundation of effective intercession. Intercession is not a JOB, it is a love relationship that develops between you and your heavenly Father. Intercession is a stethoscope to the heart of God. Our ability to hear His heart deepens with time. The more we listen to Him, the better we know Him, His works and His voice. Time in His presence will transform us. As we journey with Him beyond the veil, we will experience the priestly privilege of intercession.

Join me as I share some of my own journey beyond the veil...

### UNVEILING THE TRUTH ABOUT YOU

1. Have you fallen into the trap of making prayer a duty, a ritual or an obligation? Would you release yourself from all perceived expectations of others? Will you be patient with yourself as you learn to intercede?
2. The spiritual gifts in your life will influence what issues motivate you to intercede. What type of intercessor are you?
3. What is it about targeted united corporate intercession that makes Satan nervous? Are you willing to encourage people in your sphere of influence to appreciate the diversity of their prayer styles?
4. Do you have to be a gifted intercessor to pray effectively during corporate prayer? Does your fear cause you to emulate others rather than praying in accordance with the gifts the Holy Spirit has given you?

## Notes

1. C. Peter Wagner, *Prayer Shield* (Ventura, Calif.: Regal Books, 1992), p. 47.
2. Paul E. Holdcraft, *Cyclopedia of Bible Illustrations* (New York: Abingdon-Cokesbury Press, 1957), p. 28.
3. Wagner, *Prayer Shield*, p. 50.
4. Andrew Murray, *The Ministry of Intercession* (Springdale, Pa.: Whitaker House, 1982), p. 43.
5. Norman P. Grubb, *Rees Howell Intercessor* (Fort Washington, Pa.: Christian Literature Crusade, 1952), p. 88.
6. Mike Bickle Teaching Notes, "The True Prophetic Spirit" Holiness Unto the Lord Conference, 1990, p. 119.
7. Cyrus E. Albertson, *The Treasure Chest* (New York: Harper and Row Publishers, 1965), p. 194.
8. Andrew Murray, *The Ministry of Intercession*, p. 43.
9. Holdcraft, *Cyclopedia of Bible Illustrations*, p. 192-193.

# CHAPTER FOUR

# Priesthood of the Believer

## "PRIESTLY KINGS" AND "KINGLY PRIESTS"

I have often wondered how a man relates to being called "the Bride of Christ." It is as difficult for a woman to see herself as "a son of God." The term "priest" is also connotative of the male gender. However, years of experience and an in-depth study of the Old Testament priesthood have caused me to realize that as sanctified believers, we are all called to the role of priest.

### THE OLD TESTAMENT PRIESTHOOD

Understanding the role of the Old Testament priesthood is central to our functioning as the priests God has called us to be. Permit me to explain...

Isaiah prophesied:

> They will be called oaks of righteousness, a planting of the Lord for the display of his splendor. They will rebuild the ancient ruins and restore the places long devastated; they will renew the ruined cities that have been devastated for generations...And you will be called priests of the Lord, you will be named ministers

of our God. You will feed on the wealth of nations, and in their riches you will boast (Isa. 61:3,4,6).

Isaiah was prophesying about a new breed of priests—the priests we are to be! Priests who will *rebuild* the ancient ruins and *restore* the devastated places.

Many today who are beginning to understand their priestly roles respond only in negative language, such as tearing down strongholds, etc. Certainly that must be done. However, the priesthood God will use in this last hour of history will be more than a spiritual "wrecking crew." These priests will *rebuild, restore* and *renew!*

The Old Testament priest had several duties in the Temple. Yet Exodus 28 repeatedly says that the priest's primary duty was to minister to God:

> And take thou unto thee Aaron thy brother, and his sons with him, from among the children of Israel, that he may *minister unto me* in the priest's office...And thou shalt put the priestly garments upon Aaron thy brother, and his sons with him; and shalt anoint them, and consecrate them, and sanctify them, that they may *minister unto me* in the priest's office (vv. 1,41, *KJV*, italics added).

We can easily become so involved in the "work of the Lord" that we overlook the "Lord of the work." Our priority each morning at prayer time should be to *minister unto our Lord.* Sing to Him, brag on Him and read the Word back to Him.

The Old Testament priest was required to offer sacrifices for the sin of the people and to keep the incense burning. But the priesthood is no longer a select group, nor is it exclusively for the Israelite, the Levite, within the family of Aaron. Going beyond the veil into the Holy of Holies is no longer something one man does once a year, at the risk of his life.

Now, Jesus Christ has become the sinless sacrifice for all who would receive His remedy for sin. Today, therefore, *all* who have accepted His free gift of redemption have access to the Holy of Holies as they move beyond the veil in prayer. When these sanctified saints enter in, the fragrance of what Jesus did in conjunction with the praises and prayers of the saints becomes an incense before the Lord. They function as priests.

Peter writes, we are a "royal priesthood" (1 Pet. 2:9). We minister unto the King of kings through intimate relationship with Him. And when we do, we become His ambassadors to the world. We need to live in relationship with our Father, the King, at increasingly deeper levels so the world can see our royal priestly lives and want to know Him through our representation of Him.

## MY EARLY DAYS

I grew up in a secure family that expressed love freely and represented the Father favorably. Although I was in church from the cradle roll, my name was not written on heaven's roll until I accepted Christ as my Savior at age 15.

Our family which includes my parents, Gene and Martha Day; my older sister, JoAnn McDougal; my older brother, John Day and his twin, my sister, Martha Jean Hallmark (who went to be with the Lord on Easter in 1996) attended and served faithfully at the First Baptist Church in Lake Jackson, Texas.

It was there that Pastor Johnny Beard led me to Jesus. Jim Bob and Louverl Griffin were my music and youth directors. They demonstrated a passionate love for the Lord Jesus that created a hunger inside me to know Him.

And knowing Jesus brought answers to many of the issues I had struggled with during my youth. As a small child, I was very sensitive to the needs of others. Some said I had the gift of mercy (see Rom. 12:8). Others said I might be too melancholy and needed to be less emotional. Fortunately, when I became a Christian, God showed me that I was born to intercede! However, I had almost no understanding of this call to intercession.

During those early years, I spent many hours weeping and praying before the Lord. As questions about how to draw close to Jesus formed in my mind, I realized my prayer life was underdeveloped, so I began to collect a list of adjectives describing God. Song of Songs 1:3 says, "Your name is like perfume poured out." The devil would accuse me of being a hypocrite because I had made a list to help me express my heart to the Lord, but I ignored the enemy, refused his lies and continued to brag on Jesus. I now have more than 300 terms describing the majesty of the Lord. The following is a sampling for you to use as you compile your own love ledger:

> All Powerful • Bread of Life • Superior • Savior • Abba Father • Bridegroom • The Door to Life • Lover of My Soul • Lord • Jehovah • My Intercessor • Holy • Majestic • Gentle • Darling of My Life • Full of Mercy and Grace • Husband • King of All Ages • Joy Giver • Partner in Prayer • Apple of My Eye • Creator of All Things • Friend • Glorified One • Faithful One

I began by praying for 15 minutes a day. Eventually this time increased to 30 minutes. As my prayer life developed, so did my desire to be near to the heart of the Lord...and to be His good friend.

One day as I was casually talking with the Lord, I experienced a deep longing for a more intimate relationship with Him. In His goodness, the Lord began to introduce me to books by Andrew Murray, Rees Howells, Watchman Nee, Evelyn Christensen, Dick Eastman, A. W. Tozer and others that enriched my prayer life. Doors of opportunity opened for me to meet people who understood my spiritual quest for intimacy in prayer.

## MEETING MISS CORRIE

One significant encounter happened in 1973 when I met Corrie ten Boom, author of the best-selling book *The Hiding Place* (which was also made into a movie).

*The Hiding Place* chronicles Corrie's experiences during World War II as her family sought to protect Jewish refugees from Nazi persecution. Corrie and her family were arrested and imprisoned in a concentration camp where her entire family died. After her release from the concentration camp, Corrie traveled worldwide, emphasizing the need to forgive our enemies in the power of the Lord Jesus and to be ready for His coming.

On this cold winter night in 1973, my heart was warm with

the expectancy of meeting this prayer warrior about whom I had read so many stories. At age 23, I was inexperienced in the ways of God, but I was anxious to learn and I hoped that this divine appointment would provide insight for my spiritual growth.

Eddie and I were attending a dinner party at the home of a prominent Christian businessperson in Memphis, Tennessee. We were in town conducting a revival that week, and our host for the evening belonged to the church we were visiting. Our visit was clearly God's timing.

The ambiance was light and the house was full of people I did not know. They were standing around talking gaily, as if nothing significant were about to occur. The fire in the fireplace burned brightly and the aroma of food permeated the room. After what seemed an eternity, the doorbell rang. Through the door stepped Corrie ten Boom and her secretary/traveling companion. The atmosphere suddenly became electric, as if Corrie were being escorted by a legion of angels!

My heart fluttered while I was being introduced to this short, plump and vivacious friend of God. Following the introductions and dinner, Miss ten Boom sat in a chair to the left of the fireplace. Eddie and I were sitting directly across the room from her. I was spellbound. The flames from the fireplace danced in the dimly-lit room and the glory of God was so present that I could hardly breathe.

I watched with awe as Miss Corrie spoke. She would talk to us one minute and, glancing heavenward, would listen to the voice of the Father. She would nod and even answer Him aloud, then very naturally (and not at all religiously) resume talking with us.

I was overwhelmed! It was as though I were sitting in her prayer closet! Her words were cloaked with adoration and humility as she spoke about her heavenly Father. She told us how in the horror of a lice-infested Nazi concentration camp, she had found that "no pit was so deep, that God's grace was not deeper still." Her eyes glistened with tears when she recounted her experiences of intercession in the prison camp, as though each experience had become a nugget of gold. Miss Corrie anguished as she recalled how her faith was challenged in the midst of absolute hopelessness. Clearly I was looking into the eyes of a woman who *knew* the price of intimacy with God.

That night, by the Spirit of God, I saw the embodiment of a surrendered vessel, who through many tear-steeped years, had grown close enough to her Father in prayer to hear His very

.........................................................................

*Some Christians live as though God wrote a best-seller, the Bible, and then retired!*

.........................................................................

heartbeat. I yearned for that same kind of relationship with Him and I longed to hear His voice with the same kind of clarity as Corrie had demonstrated.

### WHO WILL LISTEN?

Jesus told us that we would hear His voice if we would only listen:

> The watchman opens the gate for him, and the sheep listen to his voice. He calls his own sheep by name and leads them out. When he has brought out all his own, he goes on ahead of them, and his sheep follow him because they know his voice. But they will never follow a stranger; in fact, they will run away from him because they do not recognize a stranger's voice (John 10:3-5).

Some Christians live as though God wrote a best-seller, the Bible, and then retired! They act as if He has left what happens here totally up to us. But the truth is that God is very active upon the earth! He is fulfilling biblical prophecy daily, finishing the work that He began. His purposes are coming to pass! He is a living, loving, relational God who speaks today! He never stopped speaking! We simply stopped listening. Do you have a yearning for God that burns so deeply within you that your soul is crying out to hear His voice?

Are you listening for the voice of the Good Shepherd? He has promised He will lead and direct you. Please do not refuse His call to intercede. Lay down your inadequacies, your fears and your doubts. It does not matter whether you do or do not have the gift of intercession—you can pray with His assurance that your prayers matter. The Shepherd knows you by name and He is speaking to you today. He wants to partner with you in His plans so you can share in His joy.

## ACCEPTING THE PRIESTLY ASSIGNMENT

Not only are we invited to partner with the Father concerning His plans for our planet, but Jesus also invites us to join Him in the ministry of intercession. Remarkably, He sets the example. Jesus, the great intercessor, "is able to save completely those who come to God through him, because he always lives to intercede for them" (Heb. 7:25). So our role is not to become intercessors *for* Christ, as much as it is to become intercessors *with* Him!

Furthermore, God chooses to work in this world in response to our prayer, even as Jesus in His humanity prayed and taught us to pray, "Your kingdom come, your will be done on earth as it is in heaven" (Matt. 6:10). This verse clearly implies that prayer is integral to establishing the kingdom of God upon the earth.

The following illustration is an impressive example of how our prayer is used to establish God's will upon the earth:

> David Brainerd, missionary to the American Indians, once found a whole tribe ready to accept Christ when he approached them. The story is that as he was praying in the woods, some Indians crept toward him to kill him. As they stealthily approached, they saw a rattlesnake glide out of the bush behind Brainerd, poise its head as if to strike, then lower its head and slip away. The incident so impressed the Indians that they were ready to accept the "Great Spirit" to whom Brainerd was praying.[1]

Is it possible that we have simply overlooked the tremendous priestly responsibility given to us in the area of intercession? I believe so.

### MIRACLE DAY IN KOREA

My visits throughout recent years to Yonggi Cho's church in Seoul, Korea, have convinced me of the tremendous priestly assignment we have to intercede. I have never seen so many people in one place who are graced with the burden of prayer. South Korean Christians enjoy a phenomenal experience in the throne room of God. The following story is about an American pastor who is one of Yonggi Cho's board members, however, I did not know that at the time the experience occurred.

In 1989, I read a book written by a pastor involved in national spiritual warfare who had been a Christian only 10 years. Though I had never met him, I knew immediately that I was to intercede for this pastor, his family and his church. A year later while I was in prayer, I sensed the Lord releasing some vital information for him.

I felt the Lord saying that a female on his staff was deceptive. Because this was a serious charge, I shared these words with my husband, Eddie, before I wrote a letter to this pastor. I did not include my return address, only my name. During a visit to Korea one year later, I learned, as Paul Harvey says, "the rest of the story."

Eddie and I were sitting in Yonggi Cho's 30,000-seat Korean church auditorium when I first met Peter Wagner who was the guest speaker at the Annual Church Growth Conference we were attending. Nine months before, while reading an article Peter had written, the Lord had spoken to my heart about praying for him daily. I was content to pray for him without ever expecting to meet him. I was accustomed to interceding for leaders I did not know. However, the Lord had a different plan.

Throughout the session Eddie and I noticed Peter looking right at us with unusual repetition. Although the auditorium was quite large, his eyes were drawn to where we were sitting.

During a break in the session, Peter approached Eddie. He recognized that Eddie was my husband and casually asked him several questions about intercession. Much to Peter's surprise,

Eddie knew the answers. He then asked Eddie if he could talk to me. Eddie curiously agreed. My back had been turned to all the activity so I had not noticed what had just transpired.

Peter addressed me while tapping me on the shoulder. As I turned and saw him standing there, I felt my face flush. He looked at me with his dark, lively, brown eyes and inquired, "You're an intercessor, aren't you?"

I nodded and nervously replied, "Yes."

Peter continued, "During the last session, the Lord pointed you out to me three times and told me you are an intercessor."

I just stood there frozen in shock, not knowing how to respond. Several of his seminary students stared at me as though expecting a reply. (Eddie said that is the only time he has ever seen me speechless!) All I could think of was the 30 years I had given to prayer, and now the Lord had revealed to a GENERAL in His prayer army that I was one in the troops! The affirmation was so overwhelming that I began to cry!

We talked briefly, then Peter returned to the platform to speak to a pastor friend. Peter reported to his friend, "You're not going to believe what just happened to me! The Lord showed me a lady in the audience, and three times He told me she is an intercessor. I just talked to her and she *is* an intercessor. She lives in Houston, Texas, and she prays for me."

The pastor asked, "Is it Alice Smith?"

Peter nodded, then asked, "How do you know Alice Smith?"

"I don't really know her," he said, "but one year ago I received a letter from a lady named Alice Smith in Houston, Texas. She shared all the details about a possible problem in our staff. She was absolutely right! Our church administrator had embezzled a large sum of money from our church and I had to fire her. After she left, our offerings increased $15,000 a week. I want to meet Alice and say thanks."

During the next break, I watched as both Peter and this pastor came down the aisle toward me. I could feel my body weaken with embarrassment! I was overwhelmed!

For many years I had prayed for leaders in the secrecy of my prayer closet. Now I was meeting two of the five men I pray for specifically! The pastor explained the complete story and I was encouraged and blessed. He asked, "Why didn't you put your return address and phone number on the letter?"

Sheepishly I admitted, "I was afraid I might be wrong."

## I-2 INFORMATION OVERLOAD

That evening Peter and his wife, Doris, asked me to become an I-2 intercessor for them. Peter Wagner defines an I-2 intercessor as one who has a casual contact with the person he or she prays for regularly. They may cross paths from time to time in other church-related events, but not much more interaction occurs between them. I agreed, of course, because it was an assignment the Lord had given me nine months earlier. This assignment was a great honor for me.

So in March of 1991, I became Peter and Doris Wagner's I-1 intercessor, who, according to Peter, is chosen by the Lord. This special relationship is based on a personal trust in the Lord and each another. Thus, for two hours that evening in Korea, Peter and Doris shared with me the miraculous events the Lord was doing around the world. They told me how God was using them. It was awesome! But I was experiencing information overload!

Later that evening when we returned to the hotel, I remembered what Leonard Ravenhill said in Kansas City during 1988:

God doesn't answer prayer, He answers desperate prayer!

I had a desperate prayer and desperately needed an answer fast! I prayed, "Lord, how can I pray about all these things Peter and Doris are doing? I don't even know where to start. I feel so inadequate."

The Lord spoke clearly to my heart, *I have called you, and I will perform My purposes through you.* Great peace flooded my heart.

## WORSHIP AND INTERCESSION: OUR PRIESTLY RESPONSIBILITIES

I realized because God had called me to the role of priest, He would also qualify me for that role as I submitted to my priestly responsibilities of worship and intercession.

In the following passage, John identifies us as priests unto God:

> Jesus Christ,...the faithful witness, the firstborn from the dead, and the ruler of the kings of the earth...who loves us and has freed us from our sins by his blood,...has made us to be a kingdom and priests (Rev. 1:5,6).

The Church today talks about the priesthood of the believer, yet knows little about it. To the average Christian, the priesthood

---

*We have been mastering the art of going to men for God, but we've never mastered the art of going to God for men.*

---

of the believer means that "nobody has a right to tell me what to do." It has become a declaration of independence rather than an answer to the call of God.

While we are knowledgeable, have respect for and are even infatuated at times with public Outer Court ministry, most believers know precious little about priestly ministry beyond the veil. We have been mastering the art of *going to men* for God, but we've never mastered the art of *going to God* for men. Perhaps this is because intercession is a closeted ministry, which offers no recognition or glory. Our labor is hidden in the closet.

Worship and intercession—"the harp and the bowl" (see Rev. 5:8)—are the priestly duties of the believer and the chief activities in heaven. John struggled to describe the worship and intercession that occurs in heaven.

> From the throne came flashes of lightning, rumblings and peals of thunder...In the center, around the throne,

were four living creatures...Day and night they never stop saying: "Holy, holy, holy is the Lord God Almighty, who was, and is, and is to come"...the twenty-four elders fall down before Him who sits on the throne, and worship Him who lives forever and ever. They lay their crowns before the throne and say: "You are worthy, our Lord and God, to receive glory and honor and power, for you created all things, and by your will they were created and have their being" (Rev. 4:5,8-11, Paraphrased).

Jesus taught us to pray that His Kingdom would come and His will be done on earth as it is being done in heaven. So what is being done in heaven? Worship and intercession! We are to pray that heavenly worship and intercession might ascend from earth to the throne, as well.

Mere words fail to describe the immeasurable joy of intimate intercession! It is heavenly! It is not of this world! While intimate intercession is happening, we move beyond the constraints of time with the Father and step into the spiritual realm of the eternal. There we gaze in wonder at the self-existent Trinity and walk away in total awe, knowing that we have not only experienced the joy of worshiping in His presence, but that we have also had the privilege of participating in a heavenly plan. These priestly responsibilities, however, are not done at our *convenience*—they are done at our *cost*!

And yet in some circles, worship and intercession are subtly subverted. They are nothing more than surface, Outer Court experiences, which are sometimes reduced to emotionalism— other times reduced to intellectualism. But these are soulish approaches to God. He is looking for those who will worship Him "in spirit and in truth." God has established the Inner Court as His meeting place. It is here that He chooses to commune with us.

David was a worshiper who experienced Inner Court worship. He wrote:

One thing I ask of the Lord, this is what I seek: that I may dwell in the house of the Lord all the days of my life, to gaze upon the beauty of the Lord and to seek him in his temple (Ps. 27:4).

Now read that passage again, noting the words "gaze upon" and "seek." Upon whom did David gaze and seek? The Lord, of course. And yet our worship and intercession often becomes focused on lesser things.

While all worship and intercession causes destruction in the enemy camp, neither worship nor intercession should become focused on Satan. They are to be "God directed." Both worship and intercession are about the Father's heart, not our problems. As we align our hearts with His, we breathe in the life of His plans and breathe out our own. We gain spiritual authority in the prayer closet as we cultivate this kind of intimacy.

And even though we will address the enemy at times, we must not let our worship and our intimate intercession become focused upon the devil and his activity. To do so degenerates the power of worship and intercession. Remember, worship and intercession are both ministries *to* God!

The word "priest" in Latin means "bridge builder." The word "priest" in Hebrew means "one who stands up for another and states his cause." The priestly role of the intercessor is "to stand in the gap for another." Israel's priests were intercessors for the nation.

As intercessors, we priestly believers today are the spiritual reality of the Old Testament priests. We must press in! It is up to us to meet the requirements for effective priestly ministry before the Lord. We have the great honor of joining hands with a victorious Lord to dispel the darkness of satanic dominion in the lives of individuals as well as nations.

We must be wise to heed the words of the apostle Peter:

But you are a chosen people, a royal priesthood, a holy nation, a people belonging to God, that you may declare the praises of him who called you out of darkness into his wonderful light (1 Pet. 2:9).

Next, we will see the divine pattern in the building of the tabernacle, which can be summed up in Exodus 25:8: "Let them make me a sanctuary that I may dwell among them" (*KJV*). This verse is the key thought of all that pertains to both the priest and the tabernacle; we are to be a habitation for the Lord. We are to live and move and breathe beyond the veil.

UNVEILING THE TRUTH ABOUT YOU

1. Do you feel awkward being called the Bride of Christ? a son of God? a spiritual priest?
2. What is the primary role of the priest? Are you living like a spiritual priest? Would the Lord say you "minister to Him"?
3. Do you have a genuine desire to know the Lord better? Are you willing to pay the price to see this happen?
4. Does God speak to you? What are the blockages that keep you from listening to Him?

**Note**
1. Paul E. Holdcraft, *Cyclopedia of Bible Illustrations* (New York: Abingdon-Cokesbury Press, 1957), Illustration 1057, p. 235.

# CHAPTER FIVE

# God's Pattern: The Tabernacle

## A HOUSE OF PRAYER

You are the temple of God!

God has used many of the historical facts that we read in Scripture to unify His Word with what is to come through "typology"—people, places and things mentioned in the Old Testament that prefigure people, places and things mentioned in the New Testament.

For example, Hebrews tells us that the tabernacle of Moses was only a shadowy, earthly outline of the true heavenly sanctuary, the real spiritual tabernacle which is fulfilled through Jesus Christ (see 8:5). And John wrote, "After this I looked and in heaven the temple, that is, the tabernacle of the Testimony, was opened" (Rev. 15:5). All of the priestly duties performed in the Old Testament tabernacle and temple were but the foreshadow of what was to come.

## CHRIST—THE TABERNACLE

Though more than one interpretation of the Old Testament tabernacle can be cited, the primary interpretation is found in the Person of the Lord Jesus Christ. Jesus angrily challenged the money changers, "Destroy this temple, and I will raise it again in three days" (John 2:19). They assumed He was talking about

Herod's temple in Jerusalem. But Jesus was actually speaking of His physical body, the earthly dwelling place of God.

And John 1:14 tells us that "the Word became flesh and dwelt among us" (*NKJV*). The Greek word "dwelt" is also translated "tabernacled." Thus, we see that Jesus not only became the tabernacle, but He also tabernacles within us.

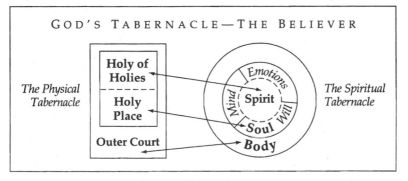

GOD'S TABERNACLE—THE BELIEVER

(Fig. 5-a)

So the secondary interpretation of the tabernacle relates to the believer. Today, we the Church, the Body of Christ, are the dwelling place of God upon earth. We are the temple of God, a house of prayer. Occasionally someone will ask, "How can I hold a secular job, maintain a family, etc., and still be a 'house of prayer?'"

The answer is: It is not where your knees touch the ground, but where your spirit is that counts! It is not the position of your body, but the condition of your heart that matters! And finally, it is not where you dwell when you pray, but WHO dwells in you that makes you a house of prayer.

God made us to live in continual communion with Him. Jesus is in heaven and the Holy Spirit is in us. When we pray, something powerful happens. Things that were only physical in the Old Testament—the temple, the brazen altar, the laver and the altar of incense, etc.—in the New Testament are described as spiritual. (See Hebrews.) You and I are the spiritual temple of God.

> Do you not know that your body is a temple of the Holy Spirit, who is in you, whom you have received from God? You are not your own; you were bought at a price. Therefore honor God with your body (1 Cor. 6:19,20).

The temple of old was a meeting place with God. The temple priests fully expected to encounter the Lord within its walls.

Today, when the world sees us, they see God's dwelling place (see 2 Cor 6:16). We have the priestly privilege of ministering to the Lord. As did these former Levites, we (spiritual Levites) should expect and experience divine encounters. "You have made them to be a kingdom and priests to serve our God, and they will reign on the earth" (Rev. 5:10).

## GOD AND GREEN BEANS

Bryan, our second son, was five years old when he gave his heart to Jesus. He was still trying to understand the idea that Jesus lives in us and we are His temple when one night at dinner, after examining his food, he asked, "Does Jesus like green beans?"

"Yes, Bryan, Jesus likes green beans. Why do you ask?" I questioned.

He answered, "Because if Jesus lives in me, He has to eat what I eat...and I wanted to make sure He likes green beans."

Smart kid! And he is right! Because we are the temple, Jesus lives with us, in us and through us.

We are tripartite beings, meaning we are comprised of three parts: *spirit*, *soul* and *body*. The Old Testament tabernacle was also tripartite. It consisted of the *Outer Court*, the *Holy Place* and the *Holy of Holies*. Nothing about the tabernacle was accidental. It was all part of a master plan. As we compare the three parts of the tabernacle, we see that they parallel the three parts of the human temple.

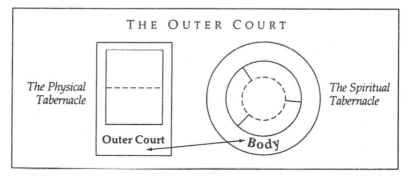

(Fig. 5-b)

The *Outer Court* represents the *body*, our outer part. (See Fig. 5-b.) Everyone sees the body, just as all could see the Outer Court of the temple. I call the body our "earth suit" because it is necessary for living on this planet.

The *Holy Place* was hidden in a tent, much like our souls (housing the mind, will and emotions) are hidden within our bodies. And the *Holy of Holies* was the most sacred place in the temple, the place where God dwelt and spoke only to the High Priest—but only once each year! (The tribes of Israel set up camp around the tabernacle. However, only a select group of priests could go inside and only the High Priest could enter the Holy of Holies.) The *human spirit* is our Holy of Holies, where God comes to live at the time of our salvation (see Rom. 8:9). And it is here that He communes with us, not once a year, but anytime!

Two-thirds of a person—the spirit and soul—are hidden. Only the body is visible. Yet most of us spend two-thirds of our time building up the one-third (our bodies) that will return to dust. Paul gave insight about spiritual realities when he said, "We look not at the things which are seen, but at the things which are not seen; for the things which are seen are temporal, but the things which are not seen are eternal" (2 Cor. 4:18, *KJV*).

It is within the mind, will and emotions (our souls) that sanctification occurs. Sanctification means to be "set apart for God." Yet our five senses (taste, hear, smell, feel and touch) often control us. When our senses are aroused, they in turn stimulate our desires. "Therefore do not let sin reign in your mortal body so that you obey its evil desires" (Rom. 6:12).

When we consistently entertain sensual or worldly soulish behavior, the process of sanctification is on hold. Once we decide to surrender our minds, wills and emotions to the Holy Spirit within us, the process of sanctification resumes. As we consider the temple, we see how God made preparation for the sanctification process to be facilitated.

The Old Testament tabernacle and temple were equipped with furniture. However, unlike the buildings and shrines of other religions, the tabernacle housed no idols or images. Why? Because God Himself dwelt there.

The first item of furniture was the brazen altar, in the Outer Court, where man began his approach to God. To the Hebrew an altar meant "a slaughter place." This brazen altar symbolized calvary's cross, where Christ was led as a lamb to the slaughter. It is at the Cross where we begin our approach to God.

(Fig. 5-c)

Paul E. Billheimer, in his book *Destined for the Throne*, describes the death of Jesus:

> It was not the prospect of physical suffering which brought the agony in the Garden. That was nothing compared to the torture of His spirit. It was the anguish of a pure soul who knew no sin, facing the injustice of being "made sin" (2 Cor. 5:21), of being so completely identified with sin as not only to forfeit the fellowship of His Father, but to become the object of the Father's loathing. This was no mere legal imputation of sin. He was made sin. He became the very essence of sin by dying as a sin offering."[1]

The victory, however, of becoming the perfect offering for sin on the cross gave Jesus the right to foreclose on the devil (see Heb. 2:14). So, the brazen altar reminds us of Christ's sacrificial death on calvary for our sins.

## DEATH TO SELF

Any discussion of the brazen altar must include not only Christ's death for us, but also our death to self (the flesh or fallen nature within us that is contrary to God). We cannot go into the Holy of

Holies until we have made the choice to sacrifice (or submit) "self." We do this as we:

- Recognize all known sin and confess it;
- Release others through forgiveness;
- Receive His forgiveness;
- Refocus on Him;
- Remember, rely on and realign with His Word;
- Regard His voice;
- Rejoice in His sacrifice.

Paul begged the Romans, "Therefore, I urge you, brothers, in view of God's mercy, to offer your bodies as living sacrifices, holy and pleasing to God" (Rom. 12:1).

Just as salvation is a "death experience" that is born out of choice, so also is the Christian life! Paul said, "I die daily" (1 Cor. 15:31, *KJV*). Thus, Paul was saying that daily he chooses God's will and by doing so sacrifices his own. When we sacrifice our wills to God, our sacrifices are pleasing to Him.

A pleasing sacrifice placed upon the brazen altar gave the priest the right to enter the most sacred place, the Holy of Holies. The writer of Hebrews assures us that Christ's perfect sacrifice qualifies us as spiritual priests to enter the Holy of Holies as well: "Since we have confidence to enter the Most Holy Place by the blood of Jesus, by a new and living way" (Heb. 10:19,20).

Jesus is "the way" (John 14:6). And because He is, all of us can pray. All of us can confess our sins. We can all offer supplication, thanksgiving and petition to the Lord.

Those considering the cost of discipleship must daily relinquish the right to self and become "spiritual Levites" whose lives delight God. However, they can only carry out the priestly function of selfless intercession within the Holy of Holies, beyond the veil, by building altars with undefiled *stones* and cultivating humility by refusing to climb the *steps*. Let me explain.

UNDRESSED STONES AND UNUSED STEPS

1. *Undressed stones.* The Lord told Moses:

Make an altar of earth for me and sacrifice on it your

burnt offerings and fellowship offerings, your sheep and goats and your cattle. Wherever I cause my name to be honored, I will come to you and bless you. If you make an altar of stones for me, do not build it with dressed stones, for you will defile it if you use a tool on it (Exod. 20:24,25).

Why do you think the Lord told Moses not to build the altar of dressed stones or build it with tools? A dressed stone is a carved stone, smoothed with man-made tools. God was warning the people that man's effort to carve smooth stones is unacceptable. Why?

First, salvation is "not of works" (see Eph. 2:8,9). The only works that satisfy God are His own. But the second reason man's effort is unacceptable is that the altar is a place of death. Only jagged, rough-hewn altar stones would resemble death. We defile the altar when we attempt to add our self-made works (education, money, reputation, service, good deeds, etc.) to His "finished work."

2. *Unused stones.* Then the Lord told Moses in verse 26:

And do not go up to my altar on steps, lest your nakedness be exposed on it.

Why no steps? Steps represent man's attempt to elevate himself. The purpose for steps is to take us higher, but James warns, "God opposes the proud but gives grace to the humble" (Jas. 4:6).

Pride was Satan's downfall. Satan said, "I will ascend to heaven; I will raise my throne above the stars of God; I will sit enthroned on the mount of assembly,...I will ascend above the tops of the clouds; I will make myself like the Most High" (Isa. 14:13,14). The center of pride is "I"; so is the center of sin. Satan had "I" trouble.

To paraphrase, God says, "Do not carve the stones of the altar, for that has everything to do with you and nothing to do with Me. Leave them rough hewn. And do not elevate yourself by using steps to approach Me at My altar."

In other words, intercession is a place of death, a place of lowliness and humility. We don't dress the stones by trying to work up a burden. This is flesh and the Lord says it is defiled. Neither should we climb steps for self-elevation by trying to look religious or wanting to be noticed.

The work of intercession must be God directed, Christ honoring and Spirit led. It is the authored and finished work of Christ who is the "author and perfecter of our faith" flowing through us (Heb. 12:2).

But before we can truly move into the fullness of His life flow, we must purify ourselves. The Old Testament priests relied on the laver for cleansing.

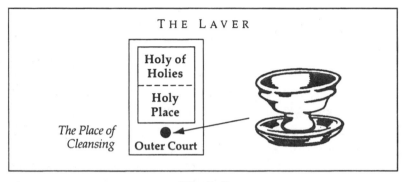

(Fig. 5-d)

The laver, a bronze bowl of water used to cleanse the priests for ministry, was the second article of furniture in the Outer Court. The bowl was made of bronze symbolizing that sin was still present. Bronze represented those things that were not yet purified or needing judgment, whereas gold represented purity.

The laver was used to teach the priests purity. The water was daily changed and the priests were required to wash before any of their ministrations. We, too, must keep our hearts and hands clean before ministering to or on behalf of God (see Ps. 24:3,4; 26:6).

The water in the basin represents God's Word which cleanses our lives from sin (see Eph. 5:26). Today therefore we must continue to stay in the Word if we are to keep sin from seeping into our lives (see 1 John 1:9).

Oswald Chambers writes in *My Utmost for His Highest*:

> If we lose the vision, we alone are responsible, and the way we lose the vision is by spiritual leakage. If we do not run our belief about God into practical issues, it is all up with the vision God has given. It is essential to practice the walk of the feet in the light of the vision.[2]

So where does the light of the vision come from? It comes from drawing closer to the presence of God. Jesus said, "I am the light of the world" (John 9:5). Spiritual light comes as we move out of the "sunlight" and into the "Son light"—as we move from the Outer Court into the Holy Place.

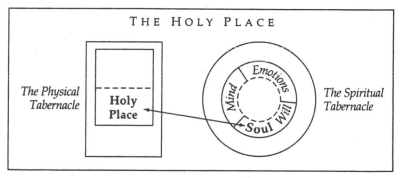

(Fig. 5-e)

The Outer Court was open to the natural light of the sun, the stars and the moon, but the Holy Place could not have any natural light. As the Outer Court symbolizes a person's body, the *Holy Place* symbolizes the *soul*—mind, will and emotions, or control tower of the body. The soul is where our choices are made that bring either greater light or darkness into our lives and those choices are based on who or what power we have allowed to be in control.

Throughout the Bible, oil has been used to represent spiritual power in the same sense that today oil is used in the world to represent financial power. Therefore, as we consider the kind of fuel used to keep the lamps burning in the Holy Place, we see that the oil parallels the Holy Spirit's power to control us as we surrender to Him.

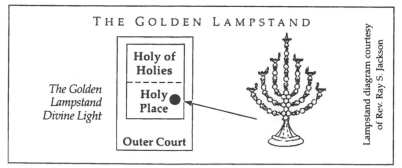

(Fig. 5-f)

The golden lampstand consisted of oil lamps, not candles. Candles burn out, but oil lamps burn the continual supply of oil being poured into them. The golden lampstand oil produced a flame symbolic of the Holy Spirit. Inside the Holy Place, the priest walked by its light, the divine light of the Spirit.

Observation, reasoning and rationalizing may be fine for natural things, but intercession is dependent upon the illumination of the Holy Spirit. The things of God are often transrational.

God used candles to illustrate this point through a family experience. One night while I was cooking, our son Bryan came into the kitchen for a snack. As he turned to leave he casually said, "Mom, you need to have some candles ready."

I asked, "Why do I need candles, Bryan?"

He replied, "We are going to have a bad storm and the lights are going to go out." (The weather outside was beautiful. There was not a cloud in the sky.)

"How do you know that? Did you hear something on TV?" I asked.

"No, I just feel the Lord has told me that we are to be ready for a storm."

Confident that he was somehow right, I found candles and set them on the counter. Less than an hour later, a huge thunderstorm and tornado roared through our neighborhood. The lights flickered and went out. The next morning broken tree limbs, roofing shingles and debris lay strewn throughout the streets.

Bryan had received this information without natural knowledge, but from divine illumination. God speaks to those who speak to Him! And our communion with Him can best be seen through the similitude of the table in the Holy Place.

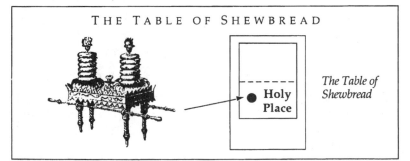

THE TABLE OF SHEWBREAD

Holy Place

The Table of Shewbread

(Fig. 5-g)

The table on which the shewbread lay was made of shittim wood, overlaid with gold. This table was the center of union and communion for the priesthood. Twelve loaves of fresh bread were placed on this table daily. The priests were to abide in the Holy Place and to eat the bread at the table (see Lev. 24:9).

The table of shewbread is a metaphor for our communion with God which comes as we fellowship with Him and eat of the Bread of Life, Jesus! Christ sustains the believer's spiritual life. Jesus declared, "I am the bread of life. He who comes to me will never go hungry, and he who believes in me will never be thirsty" (John 6:35).

The greatest joy of intercession is found in our communion and fellowship with Jesus. Inner joy bubbles up and satisfies the soul, just as bread satisfies the body. And not only are *we* gratified through intercession, but God's Word tells us that our prayer is also gratifying to *God* because it is a sweet fragrance (perfume or incense) before the Lord (see 2 Cor. 2:15). Thus, we move to the altar of incense.

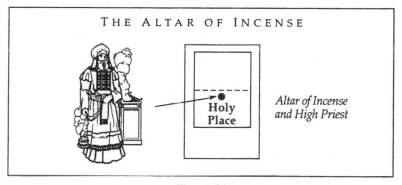

(Fig. 5-h)

The altar of incense was at the very heart of the temple. As we have clearly seen, incense is representative of intercession (see Rev. 5:8.) Therefore, the ministries of intimate intercession and praise are at the very heart of God. The altar of incense was the furnishing closest to the veil. It was nearest to the glory of God (the Ark of the Covenant). "May my prayer be set before you like incense; may the lifting up of my hands be like the evening sacrifice" (Ps. 141:2).

In the Old Testament, only the High Priest and selected

priests could minister at the altar of incense. In Christ Jesus, however, these two offices are permanently united, and we stand in the righteousness of Christ. We have become kings and priests unto God (see Heb. 10:19-22). As priestly believers, it is our great privilege to burn the incense (our intercession) before the throne of God (Rev. 5:9,10). But many today refuse to offer pure and obedient worship to Him. Instead they seek to worship on their own terms in their own ways to their own self-made gods. Be assured God does not overlook this fraudulent worship.

## STRANGE FIRE

Exodus 30:9 says, "Do not offer on this altar any other incense." The first fire on the altar was divinely lit. On the day of the dedication of the tabernacle, divine fire fell from heaven and lit the sacrifice. Coals from the divine fire on the brazen altar were used to light the altar of incense, making it divine fire (God-made). Any other fire was "strange fire." Any incense other than God's prescribed incense was "strange incense." When Korah and his company offered strange fire to God, He killed them (see Num. 16)!

Strange fire or strange incense speak of false worship—ANY worship that originates from a source other than God. Sadly, today strange fire is coming from both the Church and the world. God hates strange fire! The world substitutes strange fire hoping that God will accept them. He will not.

During a recent visit to India I was grieved to see people offering fire to one of their more than 300,000,000 Hindu gods at any given time of the day. As I watched, I knew that those offerings, given to false gods, would never fill the emptiness in the hearts of those who offered them. Instead, their lack of fulfillment only compels them to create new gods. They hope to eventually find a god that will work for them.

The cloud and smell of incense is so thick in the Hindu temples that it is stifling. And yet this blanket of incense brings no peace. God accepts only the sweet incense that originates in heaven—in His way and according to His time.

## THE TIME OF INCENSE

You might remember from Luke 1 that Zechariah and Elizabeth, John the Baptist's parents, were "righteous before God." Both were of the priestly tribe of Aaron, advanced in years, yet barren! In the same way, the Church today is a kingdom of priests (see Rev. 1:6), advanced in years, having had 2,000 years to learn the priestly skills, and yet we are essentially barren—powerless and fruitless.

Luke records that Zechariah's priestly division was assigned temple duty when he drew the lot to burn the incense (see Luke 1:8,9, *KJV*). Imagine being chosen from a pool of approximately 22,000 active priests. This was a once in a lifetime opportunity! Verse 10 tells us that as he burned the incense, multitudes of people were praying outside the temple, for it was "the time of incense."

As Zechariah burned the incense before the first coming of Jesus, I believe our generation has drawn the lot to burn the incense before Christ's second coming! Around the world, multitudes are praying! Those who burn the incense will become saturated with the fragrance of intercession that ascends pleasantly before Him. And as they do, they will experience life the way God intended it: so connected and satisfied by Him in the Holy of Holies that when people living in the Outer Court and the world experience the fragrance of His lingering presence, they will be aroused and unsatisfied with strange fire and counterfeit incense. They will long for that place known as the Holy of Holies.

(Fig. 5-i)

It is within the Holy of Holies that we find the Ark of the Covenant. The ark was made of two materials: *shittimwood,* overlaid with *gold* inside and out. The wood symbolized Christ's human nature. God promised to raise a righteous "branch" to rule over His people (see Isa. 4:2). Jesus, in an attempt to identify with us, insistently called Himself "the Son of Man."

Pure gold covered the wooden box, symbolic of His divine nature. The gold and wood together represented Christ's two natures: His humanity (see 1 Tim. 3:15,16) and His deity (see Heb. 1:3).

The Mercy Seat, adorned with golden cherubim, rested atop the ark. Psalm 80:1 says, "Hear us, O Shepherd of Israel,...you who sit enthroned between the cherubim, shine forth." His presence made the Ark of the Covenant the most significant piece of furniture in the tabernacle.

In the same way, His presence must be at the center of all individual and corporate worship today. Without the presence of the Lord, ritual and prayer are meaningless. If the presence of the Lord is not resting on a church, it operates in the strength of the flesh and becomes a mere empty facade.

Second Chronicles 5:13,14 gives an account of God's glory filling the temple that Solomon built. The cloud of God's presence so filled the room that the priests could not even stand to perform their service! The goal of our worship should be that we get to the place where we do not see anyone or anything around us. Instead, we are completely consumed with the glory of His presence!

The Ark of the Covenant rested in the holiest of all, or the Holy of Holies! Once a year the High Priest would sprinkle the blood of atonement on the Mercy Seat atop the ark for the cleansing of the nation of Israel. The High Priest could never enter beyond the veil into the Holy of Holies without the blood. God said, "There, above the cover between the two cherubim that are over the ark of the Testimony, I will meet with you" (Exod. 25:22).

By the blood of Jesus, the Throne of Judgment has become a Throne of Grace! Holy God is righteous and just. When Israel broke the law of God, the people came under His divine judgment. Sin must be judged to satisfy the requirements of God's holiness. "The wages of sin is death" (Rom. 6:23). The blood-sprinkled Mercy Seat testified that a death had occurred. Once the blood was applied to the Mercy Seat, God's outraged holiness was satisfied, and His mercy was again extended.

Under the old covenant, God accepted the blood of a spotless animal as atonement for sin, symbolizing the sinless blood of Christ. Jesus is the propitiation (translated "mercy seat" in Heb. 9:5) for all who believe on Him. Christ has taken His blood into heaven's throne room. There He has sprinkled it on the Mercy Seat on our behalf, once for all!

And there is more.... Notice the name, "Mercy Seat." This is the only seat in the temple! No person other than Christ ever sat on it!

> Day after day every priest *stands* and performs his religious duties....But when this priest {Jesus} had offered for all time one sacrifice for sins, he sat down at the right hand of God (Heb. 10:11,12, italics added).

The fact that Jesus sat down is proof of His *finished work*. With judgment for our sin behind us and the mercy of God before us, Paul gives the following blessing:

> Having therefore, brethren, boldness to enter into the holiest by the blood of Jesus, by a new and living way, which he hath consecrated for us, through the veil, that is to say, his flesh; and having an high priest over the house of God; let us draw near with a true heart in full assurance of faith, having our hearts sprinkled from an evil conscience, and our bodies washed with pure water (Heb. 10:19-23, *KJV*).

Intercessors, this is your invitation! Boldly enter the throne room, because of Christ's blood. Draw near with a sincere heart, full of faith. He hears when you ask for intimacy with Him! With full assurance of faith, you can stand in the place of intercession for things that others say are impossible! Little is much when given to the Lord! Listen to His promise...

> Arise, shine, for your light has come, and the glory of the Lord rises upon you. See, darkness covers the earth and thick darkness is over the peoples; but the Lord rises upon you and his glory appears over you. Nations

will come to your light and kings to the brightness of your dawn...you will look and be radiant, your heart will throb and swell with joy (Isa. 60:1-3,5).

Beloved, this is life beyond the veil! This is what will happen when we become a house of prayer. Should we settle for less?!

## UNVEILING THE TRUTH ABOUT YOU

1. What does "tabernacle" mean? Why would the Father choose to have a physical tabernacle/temple in the Old Testament? How does the physical tabernacle/temple make us spiritual tabernacles/temples today?
2. What are the three parts of the tabernacle/temple? What are the three parts of you? To which of the three parts of you do you give the most attention?
3. God ordered Moses to specifically design the furniture for the tabernacle. What were the articles of furniture in the tabernacle? How do they relate to your life?
4. What was significant about the Altar of Incense? Was this a physical picture of what He wants your prayers to be?
5. The veil of the New Testament temple was torn in two from top to bottom (see Matt. 27:51). Why is this significant to every believer? to the intercessor? Are you taking advantage of the privilege we have to go beyond the veil in prayer?

Notes
1. Paul E. Billheimer, *Destined for the Throne* (Fort Washington, Pa.: Christian Literature Crusade, 1975), pp. 77-78.
2. Oswald Chambers, *My Utmost for His Highest* (New York: Dodd, Mead and Company, 1935), p. 71.

# *Launching Out*

## D E V E L O P I N G   C H A R A C T E R

~~~

I looked for a man [woman, teenager or child] among them who would build up the wall and stand before me in the gap on behalf of the land so I would not have to destroy it, but I found none (Ezek. 22:30).

Arise Church! Heaven is summoning you! God is forming an "end times" army of believers who will fight against the advancing enemy by standing in the gap.

Permit me to explain...

## S T A N D I N G   I N   T H E   G A P

The word "gap" in Hebrew is *perets*, which translated means "a breaking forth." In times of war, when the enemy's assault left gaps in the city walls, leaders defended their cities by standing in the broken areas of the walls for their people.

The prophets and priests in Ezekiel's day, however, would not spiritually stand in the "gap" by encouraging the people to repent, humble themselves and turn to God; therefore God had to bring judgment.

Today we can still cite many breaches in the wall. Thus, God is calling for an army of people who have counted the cost and are ready to fight. He is enlisting recruits who will suffer through the boot camp of character development in order to maintain a lifelong front-line Kingdom assault against His enemy.

"Gap standing" is difficult. It requires qualities such as humility, compassion, patience, integrity, servanthood, purity and intimacy. These traits are birthed out of death, uncelebrated in process and developed over time. Let's consider them together as we count the cost for each one.

## HUMILITY: THE LOW ROAD

Jesus cautioned, "If anyone desires to come after Me, let him deny himself, and take up his cross daily, and follow Me" (Luke 9:23, *NKJV*). No other verse more succinctly delineates the meaning of humility: "modest, lowly, defering to others."

"An official in India painted a graphic word picture of humility with his response to a complaining landowner, 'I can make your field richly fruitful if only it lies low enough.' He meant that the land could be irrigated if it wasn't too high."[1] God can make any life fruitful if it is low enough, because God uses the humble—those who will defer to Him.

Humility is bringing all that you are under His control. It is becoming God-dependent. This kind of thinking is contrary to the world's mind-set, which promotes independence and self at the center of all that can be controlled.

Jesus' beloved disciple John said, "He must become greater; I must become less." But society demands that we march in cadence with the materialistic Joneses who are always striving to "one up" us.

It is not popular today to appear weak or lacking in anything. Americans like big cars, big diamonds and big homes with big mortgages! This mega mentality has even crept into the Church. We are busy building mega buildings for our mega churches so we can preach to mega-sized crowds. Love for numbers often replaces love for people.

Instant food, ATMs, cyberspace technology, microwaves and fax machines contribute to our struggle to manufacture instant humility. But humility is largely a result of maturity, which takes both time and experience. The road to maturity is dotted with potholes that are designed to keep us humble and teachable (see Heb. 5:14).

The apostle Paul wrote:

> Are they servants of Christ? (I am out of my mind to talk like this.) I am more. I have worked much harder, been in prison more frequently, been flogged more severely, and been exposed to death again and again. Five times I received from the Jews the forty lashes minus one. Three times I was beaten with rods, once I was stoned, three times I was shipwrecked, I spent a night and a day in the open sea, I have been constantly on the move. I have been in danger from rivers, in danger from bandits, in danger from my own countrymen, in danger from Gentiles; in danger in the city, in danger in the country, in danger at sea; and in danger from false brothers. I have labored and toiled and have often gone without sleep; I have known hunger and thirst and have often gone without food; I have been cold and naked (2 Cor. 11:23-27).

Paul was challenging the pride of the Corinthians by explaining that his life in ministry was in total contrast to their assumptions.

We often make the same wrong assumptions today. When we pray, "Lord, use me," this is usually a request to be lifted up. But in God's economy, we are really praying, "Lord, change me," though we may not know it. He changes us by bringing us into a place of lowliness. Jonathan Edwards said, "Nothing sets a person so much out of the devil's reach as humility."

And nothing is more effective in developing humility than failure. "During a lecture when a particular experiment failed to 'come off,' Lord Kelvin, a British science professor, addressed his students, 'Gentlemen, when you are face-to-face with a difficulty, you are up against a discovery.' This applies not only in science but also in personal living."[2]

Difficult experiences test us. They show us where we need to make changes and what we need to learn. Disappointments are His appointments. They teach us how to trust. Jesus is bringing many sons and daughters to Himself and He will not shield us from the requirements of sonship. When trouble comes, we have the opportunity to either humble ourselves before God or lift ourselves up with pride and resistance.

The path toward humility is trodden through death to self. When self is dead, humility has been perfected (see Gal. 2:20). Jesus humbled Himself unto death, and by His example the way is opened for us to follow.

........................................................

*The person who is offended by the words of others only proves that death to self has not been finished.*

........................................................

A dead man or woman does not react to an offense. The truth is that the person who is offended by the words of others only proves that death to self has not been finished.

Do you want to know how far you have come on the path toward humility? You will find the answer in your reaction to the last offense you experienced. When you humble yourself with perfect peace of heart despite injustice, then death to self is complete. Death is the seed; humility is the ripened fruit.

## BUILDING CHARACTER BY BREAKING PRIDE

Humility is cultivated in the classroom of humiliation. I began to learn this lesson as a young person, and my experiences in brokenness occasionally caused me to question my heavenly Instructor's intentions.

In school I was very popular. Among other honors, I was the class favorite, a member of the student council and a cheerleader. But after I trusted Christ as my Savior, word spread throughout the school that I had "gotten religion"! My pride was severely tested when some friends shoved me against a locker and called me a "street corner preacher." They said my religion would never last. Trying to bring discouragement, they said in a short amount of time I would not love God as much as I did then. They were right! Today, I love Him more!

But it was difficult standing against peer pressure and at times I felt confused and hurt. I loved the Lord enough to hang in there and I did. I know now that my friends were threatened by the change in my life. One by one my honors and then my popularity disappeared. But I trusted the Lord to do whatever He needed to do to build His character into me.

The process of character building involves a word that most people do not like to hear: "failure." Some believers frantically go to great lengths to hide it, or to rationalize it away! In doing so, however, they are resisting the Father's main instrument used to conform them into the likeness of His Son!

God used failure to reveal my need for total dependence upon Him. The spring of my sophomore year in high school, I lost the cheerleader election. With rising frustration, I lost a student council position due to a mistake in counting the votes. My junior and senior years I lost the All-State championship for best soprano vocalist. As a 16-year-old, those were traumatic days!

I had grown up in a secure, stable Christian home, rarely missing church services, however, I do not recall hearing any sermons teaching that brokenness could be my best friend. Scripture has much to say about the necessity for brokenness; still it was not popular to preach that "we share in his sufferings in order that we may also share in his glory" (Rom. 8:17).

During my senior year in high school, I was chosen to play the lead part in the school's stage production, "The Music Man." In my hometown, the annual musical was a big event. I was excited! Now I thought, *Everyone will see how talented I am!* Then, three weeks before the production, I became deathly ill with mononucleosis. I was in bed for three weeks. I not only missed the musical, but I was also too sick to go to most senior-class events. Some nights I would cry, "What are you doing, Lord?" I even questioned the Lord's plan for my life. The downward spiral of failure continued into my college and early years of ministry.

After Eddie and I married, we traveled in full-time evangelism, living on the gracious love offerings of small churches. It was not easy. We bought our first home with one dollar down on a VA loan. On the day escrow closed, Eddie was embarrassed: he had to borrow a dollar from the realtor for the down payment! Neither of us had one—we were broke! We slept on the floor and kept our clothes in boxes for six months because we had no furniture. Those were great times! But the breaking process continued...

By 1971, Eddie and I had lost our first baby. As a young married couple we did not have insurance, and I was left to sit in the admissions office of the hospital in pain and grief, bleeding, while Eddie found money to pay the hospital for my treatment.

We bought a motor home in 1972 so we could travel more freely. At a Houston revival, however, our two-week-new motor home was stolen. We had already sold our permanent home and furniture. All that we owned was literally the clothes on our backs.

Pictures, clothing, school diplomas, jewelry and all our business and personal possessions were gone. Gone also were all the Christmas presents we had purchased for our families. And just the week before, Eddie was given a beautiful and expensive classical guitar that was also stolen. Each night for 30 days, I struggled in prayer as I could not resist the question, Why?

Finally after about three weeks, I realized it was my proud heart resisting the work of God in my circumstances. One month later, we received a call from the police that our motor home had been found, stuck in the mud on a rice farmer's field. The two men who had taken it had stripped the inside. They burned everything they could not sell. Our Bibles were all that remained.

"That was the work of the devil," you might say.

"Dear One," as our precious friend, the late evangelist Manley Beasley would say, "The devil is God's messenger boy!" God was using His messenger boy to reduce us to something He could use!

## REDUCED FOR THE MASTER'S USE

I began to experience in my prayer time the sweetness of brokenness produced by meekness and humility.

By 1973, God had revealed that He could direct my interces-

sion because the smaller I am as a broken woman, the more room
I have for Him. "The sacrifices of God are a broken spirit; a bro-
ken and contrite heart, O God, you will not despise" (Ps. 51:17).
I hung on to that promise and so can you.

Humility is an attitude of the heart, not words from the
mouth. Through our experiences with failure, we learn to submit
to the Lordship of Jesus Christ. Humility is more than saying, "I
surrender all"—it is surrendering all. There can only be one Lord.
All else must defer. And that deferment will come through a
process, a pathway of persistence.

### PERSISTENCE: REFUSING TO QUIT

Having a football coach for an earthly father set me on the path
to the persistence my heavenly Father would require from me as
an intercessor. The word "quit" was not in my vocabulary. We
grew up on quotes such as, "A winner does not quit; a quitter
does not win." The heavenly Father says:

> Ask and it will be given to you; seek and you will find;
> knock and the door will be opened to you. For everyone
> who asks receives; he who seeks finds; and to him who
> knocks, the door will be opened (Matt. 7:7,8).

A persistent intercessor is one who stands firm in spite of
interference or opposition. He or she gets ahold of a promise of
God and intercedes until the promise becomes reality.

At times even a verse can get ahold of us, and if we persist
God will eventually give us revelation. This was the case as I
struggled with Matthew 11:12:

> And from the days of John the Baptist until now the
> kingdom of heaven suffereth violence, and the violent
> take it by force (KJV).

In my mind, this radical verse never seemed to fit the rest of
the chapter. But after years of pursuing God about it, the Lord
has given me the following understanding.

## TAKING THE KINGDOM BY FORCE

Looking at the verse in its context, we find that two disciples of John the Baptist came to ask Jesus if He were the promised Messiah. John the Baptist was in prison, facing death and needing the assurance that he had fulfilled God's plan. Jesus answered the disciples by saying, "The blind receive their sight, and the lame walk, the lepers are cleansed, and the deaf hear, the dead are raised up, and the poor have the gospel preached to them" (v. 5, *KJV*).

Jesus continued by bragging about John the Baptist. He said John is the greatest among men, however, "he that is least in the kingdom of heaven is greater than he" (v. 11).

Then Jesus quoted this radical verse: "And from the days of John the Baptist until now the kingdom of heaven suffereth violence, and the violent take it by force."

The word "suffers" is the Greek word *biazo*, which means "to force, to crowd or to press forward into something." The word "violent" is the Greek word *biastes*, meaning "one who is an energetic and aggressive taker of something; even to seize or catch." So this verse is saying, "And from the days of John the Baptist until now the kingdom of heaven is *gotten by force and they that thrust men take it by force*." Jesus warns, "He that hath ears to hear, let him hear" (v. 15, *KJV*).

Jesus was saying that the radical John the Baptist was a forerunner of how the kingdom of heaven must be taken. And not just John, but even the youngest believer can intercede to rescue souls from the kingdom of darkness by thrusting the enemy's "strong holders" aside to make clearance for souls to get into the kingdom of God.

This is how it works...

My daddy was a football coach. Every day in training, his boys would line up, lower their shoulders and run into a blocking sled. My dad would often be standing on the rim of the sled adding to the weight that the boys had to push against. Above the grunts and groans, you could hear my daddy shouting, "Push, John, push. You're not pushing! Come on and give it all you've got! Get your shoulders down into that pad and shove."

This football maneuver is what Jesus was describing. Intercessor, believer, Christian, if we want to see people coming out of darkness and into the kingdom of God, then we must shove the enemy out of the way so those who are held in bondage can make the choice to enter the safety zone God has established for them. Through intercession, we must labor, force and take the Kingdom message behind enemy lines for our Coach by persevering in violent, forceful prayer. Satan is not going to hand souls over to us without resistance. No! We must press forward and aggressively take them from him by clearing the pathway of escape for his hostages.

This kind of intercession requires hard work...which brings us to another interesting verse in this same eleventh chapter of Matthew. Verse 28 says, "Come unto me, all ye that labor and are heavy laden, and I will give you rest" (*KJV*). For too long we have used this verse to deal with our stress, financial problems and relational difficulties; but let's dissect it to understand its deeper meaning.

The word "labor" expresses a continuous and repeated action. "Heavy laden" suggests an overburdened load saddled on an animal. The word "rest" translates as one offering refreshment by giving a drink of water. Therefore, I believe this verse is describing those of us who will be in the battle of violent, forceful prayer for the souls of humanity. Intercession is work! It is labor! Jesus was not removing the reality of aggressive warfare and labor for the kingdom of God to advance. He was telling them that the dynamic, forceful warfare required to overcome the gates of hell leaves an intercessor sapped of his or her strength. So in the midst of the labor and travail for souls, come apart, rest for a time and have a drink of living water before returning to the work of laboring for souls.

In the midst of our labor, He wants to make sure that we are cared for, because He is a caring God whose heart is filled with compassion.

## COMPASSION: THE HEART OF INTERCESSION

When he saw the crowds, he had compassion on them, because they were harassed and helpless, like sheep without a shepherd (Matt. 9:36).

Compassion is suffering with someone or experiencing that person's hurt with a desire to alleviate it through some form of action. Whereas sympathy deals with emotional caring, compassion puts action behind the caring feelings.

Have you ever been sitting in your car during a red light, watching people cross the street in front of you, and wept as you experienced God's care for them? Compassion is what compels you to pray.

The Holy Spirit desires to share His heart with you. You need only be open. He grieves over every lost soul, and He is looking for those who will not only feel for the needs of others but also put those feelings into action through prayer. Compassion is the "heart" of intercession.

As we discovered earlier in this book, God often parallels those things that are happening in the physical body with those things that are happening in the spiritual realm. Sometimes I experience a dull ache in my heart for lost people. When that happens, I try not to focus on the symptom. Instead I just recognize the sign the Lord gives that prompts me to intercede for them.

Author A. J. Gordon said, "I have long since ceased to pray, 'Lord, have compassion on a lost world.' I remember the day and the hour when I seemed to hear the Lord rebuking me for making such a prayer. He seemed to say to me, 'I have had compassion on a lost world, and now it is time for you to have compassion.'"[3]

Interceding for others is one of the most compassionate things we can do for them. And Paul tells us that the Holy Spirit will help us to pray:

> In the same way, the Spirit helps us in our weakness. We do not know what we ought to pray for, but the Spirit himself intercedes for us with groans that words cannot express. And he who searches our hearts knows the mind of the Spirit, because the Spirit intercedes for the saints in accordance with God's will (Rom. 8:26,27).

In the book of Colossians, Paul himself displayed this kind of compassion. "We always thank God, the Father of our Lord Jesus Christ, when we pray for you" (Col. 1:3). Paul said he continually prayed (see v. 9), giving himself no rest. In verse 24, he said,

"Now I rejoice in what was suffered for you." The Greek word for suffering is *pathema*, meaning "pain, passion or emotion." Paul rejoiced in passionate, emotional intercession on behalf of the Colossians.

In his book *The Last of the Giants*, George Otis, Jr. tells the true story of the conversion of nearly 450 Muslim villagers in the North African nation of Algeria. George writes:

> According to testimony, on one unforgettable night in 1983—with no prior warning and for no immediately discernible reason—God sovereignly descended upon this coastal township with gracious bounty. Moving from house to house, and communicating through a combination of dreams, visions and angelic visitations, God did not rest until every member of this Muslim community was properly introduced to His only begotten Son, Jesus. As might be expected, come daybreak, nearly every villager had a story to tell.[4]

The mission workers, who did not work among these people, were curious about the reason for this visitation. They discovered an incredible piece of history. It was at this very location that, in June of 1315, Raymond Lull, a Spanish missionary, had been stoned to death by angry Muslims after he had been preaching in the open market. Otis continues:

> The blood of martyrs, it has often been said, represents the seed of the Church. In his book *The Tree of Life*, Raymond Lull wrote that Islamic strongholds are best conquered "by love and prayers, and the pouring out of tears and blood."[5]

I can visualize Raymond Lull, in those final moments as his blood moistened the ground, asking the Father one last time for the souls of this village. We serve a faithful and compassionate God. Who would have considered that nearly 700 years later the Father would have answered the prayer of Raymond Lull?

When I began to see my need to start surrendering everything to the Lord, I was at a crisis. I remember telling the Lord I would die for Him, clean toilets for Him and do anything else He might require of me. To my surprise, He asked me if I would be willing to fail for Him. At the time, I didn't see how my failure could glorify Him. I had attempted to spend my life succeeding for Him so it was difficult to understand the logic in this strange request. I have since found that human logic is of little interest to God. Reluctantly, I said, "Yes, Lord."

That yes has changed by life. It has caused me to lean on His understanding (see Prov. 3:5,6), and taught me that when I walk in obedience to the voice of our compassionate Lord, He truly does "cause all things to work together for our good" (see Rom. 8:28).

Now I ask you, have you deliberately committed your life to Jesus? If so, are you relying on who He is or who you are to qualify you for His use? As Christians we often feel that our value to God is found in our knowledge, our expertise, our money or our service. The truth is: Any old donkey will do! Not that He looks at us as such, but that the Father wants to teach us obedience in the things of the Spirit. If our *knowledge of* Him is more important to us than our *relationship with* Him, then we are not in a place where the Lord will release His compassion through us.

Paul exhorts us to "Rejoice with those who rejoice; mourn with those who mourn" (Rom. 12:15). As we demonstrate this kind of compassion, the world will know that we are His and they, too, will long to know Him. A preacher said it well, "When God measures a Christian, He puts a tape around the heart instead of the head."

Compassion is truly the heart of intercession, and this quality is developed as we invest time in His presence, trusting that our "times are in your hands" (Ps. 31:15).

PATIENCE: OBEDIENCE TO THE
HOLY SPIRIT'S TIMING

But if we hope for what we do not yet have, we wait for it patiently (Rom. 8:25).

A very difficult part of intercession is patiently waiting for answers to our prayers, especially when prayer is being used to cultivate the spiritual soil in a person's life to receive Jesus Christ as Savior. When I receive a revelation from the Lord that a person is lost, I must wait for the work of the Holy Spirit to prepare that person's heart for the gospel. First Timothy 1:16 reminds me:

> But for that very reason I was shown mercy so that in me, the worst of sinners, Christ Jesus might display His unlimited patience as an example for those who would believe on Him and receive eternal life.

When the Lord reveals that someone in the church needs salvation, He reveals it so we will pray for them. And this knowledge is to be kept in the prayer closet until the right time.

Throughout nearly 30 years of ministry the Lord has often shown Eddie and me that even though many of the dear people in the churches we have visited are serving as deacons, pastors or church leaders, they are not necessarily born again.

*Salvation is more than a marriage certificate that entitles you to bear His name; it is a love relationship that spills over into everthing you say and do.*

Many people have walked an aisle, signed a decision card, joined a church and even prayed a prayer. Some have been baptized, ordained, even confirmed, but were never saved. Some might argue that they did not know what they were doing. It may have been they knew what they were doing, but that the person who counseled with them did not know what he or she was doing.

It is difficult to understand how someone can be in church for years and not have a real conversion experience. But the Bible says the reason this occurs is that Satan has veiled the mind (see 2 Cor. 4:3,4). It happens more than you think!

Recently I was privileged to lead a friend to the Lord. She had been a devoted church member. She had faithfully served God for years...but she was lost. Many counselors had been unable to help her fill the emptiness. The harder she tried, the more frustrated she found herself. Penny said that when she read the Bible, it was a dead book. Prayer was laborious and dull. She sought to convince herself that more Bible study, more prayer and more service would fill her emptiness.

This kind of religious experience is like being married without falling in love with your spouse. You go through the motions, but the relationship is void of the intimacy that makes the two become one. Salvation is more than a marriage certificate that entitles you to bear His name; it is a love relationship that spills over into everthing you say and do. Salvation is a matter of the heart, not a matter of the head.

The Lord revealed to me that Penny was lost. She had all the head knowledge she needed, but God wanted to change her heart. Eventually Penny came for advice. This was an open door for me to suggest that she evaluate her salvation. Paul wrote:

> Examine yourselves to see whether you are in the faith; test yourselves. Do you not realize that Christ Jesus is in you—unless, of course, you fail the test? (2 Cor. 13:5).

The fact that a person is reluctant to examine himself or herself should be a red flag. True eternal life can stand the test! Within two weeks, the Lord revealed to Penny that she had never become a Christian. She was religious, but lost. Penny was saved three weeks later. Jesus is patient. He does not give up on us. I know Penny Jackson rejoices in this thought today!

## THE ASSIGNMENT

When the Lord reveals that I am to pray for someone such as I did for Penny, I write that person's name and the date in my small prayer book. Then when the Lord brings the victory, I record the date. This is my assignment record.

My job is not to confront or accuse people; my job is to exercise faith with sustained patience until the Lord brings them genuine revelation unto salvation.

You may be thinking, *Who are you to judge others?*

The answer is that I do not judge them! I do not mention anyone's condition to the Lord, He mentions it to me! I merely fulfill the prayer assignments He gives me. I keep them in the secret place of my heart until the Holy Spirit does the work.

Salvation will come if I have been hearing the Lord correctly. But part of my assignment will be to give God time.

A story is told about a woman whose face was scarred severely in a fire. Badly disfigured, it was difficult to believe she had once been quite beautiful. She and her husband had a demanding little daughter who was unhappy and embarrassed by the grotesquely scarred face of her mother. With shocking insensitivity, the heartless child reserved all affection from her mother. She refused to be seen with her mother in public and would not bring her friends home to play.

The troubled mother quietly grieved over their relationship while the daughter became more cruel and more distant with age.

Not long after the young woman had gone off to college, her mother became seriously ill and lay dying. The father called their only child home to say goodbye to her mother.

Aware of his daughter's obvious anger for being inconvenienced, her father stopped the young woman outside the door of the hospital room. He said, "I think it's about time that you know something. Your mother has always been gracious and understood your feelings about her condition. She knew you were embarrassed to be with her. All these years she has made me promise not to tell you the truth about her scars. Now I think you need to know.

"When you were only six months old, our house caught on fire. You are so pretty, and you look just like your mother once did. She could not bear the thought of losing you. Willing to lay down her life for yours, she broke through the arms of the firefighters, entered the burning house and rescued you. Tears coursed down the melting skin of her face as she emerged from that raging inferno severely burned and forever disfigured. However, your mother was overjoyed that you were safe and unharmed. Maybe now you can understand why she did not want you growing up feeling guilty every time you looked into her marred face."

The heartbroken young woman stood trembling outside the door of her dying mother's hospital room. Memories of the ugly words she had spoken raced through her mind. She could not erase the pain she had caused her mother by ignoring her and even laughing at her in front of others. For the first time, she understood how her mother had suffered for her sake.

As the young woman walked into the room, her mother appeared as pale as the sheets on which she lay. The grieving girl threw herself across her mother. She cried, "Mother, I'm so sorry! Can you ever forgive me? I never knew how much you loved me and what you suffered for me. I'm so ashamed!"

Freely she kissed her mother's face. For 20 years, the mother had waited patiently for her daughter's love. With a faint smile of joy the mother whispered, "Honey, I've already forgiven you."

If the Father requires this kind of patience from us before we see His glory, will we accept the assignment?

## INTEGRITY: WALKING THE TALK

If we accept an assignment from God, we can be sure that He will attempt to build integrity into our lives. I love Psalm 26:11,12: "But I lead a blameless life; redeem me and be merciful to me. My feet stand on level ground; in the great assembly I will praise the Lord."

My paraphrase would read:

> In all my public trust I will walk uprightly and pay strict attention to truth, honesty, justice and mercy. I will not plan evil schemes or use myself to promote my own cause. I will be true to the integrity of the Word. I will live a moral life in private and in public. I stand firmly on principles of proper conduct and I will not turn aside.

If Christians were to adopt this motto, we would not have as many cases of immorality in leadership and ministry. However, because we do, believers should be asking God for repentance and restoration on behalf of these people. Galatians 6:1 reminds us that "if someone is caught in a sin, you who are spiritual should restore him gently. But watch yourself, or you also may be tempted. Carry each other's burdens, and in this way you will fulfill the law of Christ." We are not judges; we are family.

The Lord wants each of us to have impeccable character. We should live sanctified (set apart) lives. We are to be set apart from the world. We are to be set apart to Christ. The Lord will test our integrity. We must prove to the world that we have chosen undivided loyalty to Jesus Christ. Whereas purity is developed in the prayer closet; integrity is proven in the "down and dirty world."

Integrity is meaningless until tested. Christians often think they have integrity, only to discover through their actions that it is sorely lacking. Then in brokenness, they approach the Lord with their appalling lack of integrity, and He is finally free to give them the gift of His integrity!

## JOSEPH, A MAN OF INTEGRITY

Joseph was a man of unparalleled integrity. He was apparently a handsome young man with prophetic gifts that provoked jealousy among his brothers. Motivated by their jealousy, his brothers sold him to the Midianites for what would amount to about $12.80 in today's U.S. currency. The Midianites in turn sold Joseph to Potiphar, an officer of the Pharaoh.

The story is told in Genesis 39. We read:

> When his master saw that the Lord was with him [Joseph] and that the Lord gave him success in everything he did, Joseph found favor in his eyes and became his attendant. Potiphar put him in charge of his household, and he entrusted to his care everything he owned (vv. 3,4).

However, the Lord tested Joseph's integrity before releasing him to greater levels of revelation and responsibility. Could Joseph prove faithful in the things of the world? The wife of Potiphar was the next test for Joseph:

> One day he went into the house to attend to his duties,

and none of the household servants were inside. She caught him by his cloak and said, "Come to bed with me!" But he left his cloak in her hand and ran out of the house (vv. 11,12).

This was the second time Joseph's coat had caused him trouble. The first time involved the "coat of many colors," given to him by his father. His brothers had used that coat, stained with goats' blood, and a lie, to cover up their sin. Here, Potiphar's wife used Joseph's coat to unjustly accuse him.

The master's wife punished Joseph by trying to discredit him for spurning her advances. She reported the lie to her husband and Joseph was cast into prison unjustly. There are times when we are not to fight, but to stand and see the redemption of our God. The Lord will even use the framework of injustice to develop maturity in our lives.

This happened with Joseph. But afterwards God placed him as administrator to an entire nation. He had paid the price. He understood the cost. The coats that had caused him to be unrighteously accused were replaced with robes of honor in the presence of the king. Our King also stands waiting to cover us with His regal robes of honor, but as we see in Joseph's story, the robes will come through tests and trials over time. We get integrity like E. F. Hutton said, "the old-fashioned way. We must earn it!"

## SERVANTHOOD: GOD'S METHOD FOR SUCCESS

The biblical basis for what we earn will come through servanthood. Paul speaking of Jesus said, "[He] made himself nothing, taking the very nature of a servant, being made in human likeness. And being found in appearance as a man, he humbled himself and became obedient to death—even death on a cross!" (Phil. 2:7,8).

An intercessor must be a servant. Servanthood, however, goes against our nature. We prefer to be served. Oswald Chambers asked:

Suppose God wants to teach you to say, "I know how to

be abased" are you ready to be offered up like that? Are you ready to be not so much as a drop in a bucket, to be so hopelessly insignificant, that you are never thought of again in connection with the life you served? Are you willing to spend and be spent; not seeking to be ministered to, but to minister? Some saints cannot do menial work and remain saints because it is beneath their dignity."[6]

Jesus taught that to win, we must lose; to live, we must die; to receive, we must give. To be the greatest in Christ's kingdom, we must be servants of all. Being a servant in prayer is essential to Kingdom work because God tells us to "Devote yourselves to prayer, being watchful and thankful" (Col. 4:2). The hiddenness of the prayer closet is uniquely suited for the servant hearted.

When I think of servanthood, our oldest son comes to mind. Robert is a deeply committed young husband and father. He is a songwriter and worship leader. I am proud of the testimony of servanthood he has established throughout the years.

Although Robert functions in ministry from the platform, most of his real service is done in secret. To serve unnoticed and without fanfare is greatness. God continues to give Robert intimate worship songs to write, and as He does Robert's servant heart is released as he leads congregations into the presence of the Lord. Obviously, Robert has settled in his heart the desire to serve the living God. In time, the Father who sees in secret will reward him openly!

## PURITY: UNSOILED BY THE WORLD'S SPOIL

Like Robert, we must settle in our hearts whom we will serve: this world or the kingdom of God. (See Romans 6.) If we choose God, then we have a responsibility to "set an example for the believers in speech, in life, in love, in faith and in purity" (1 Tim. 4:12).

"A man was engaged in washing a plate glass window. He did a fine job except for one spot. He rubbed that spot, used soap on it, but he could not clean the spot away. A bystander, noticing his dilemma, said, 'Sir, that spot is on the inside.'"[7] In the same way, certain "spots" in our character can only be cleansed from within!

You may be wondering: *What is a pure heart? Why is it impor-tant? And how can I have one?* The answer is found in Psalms 24:3,4:

> Who may ascend the hill of the Lord? Who may stand in his holy place? He who has clean hands and a pure heart, who does not lift up his soul to an idol or swear by what is false.

Simply put, a pure heart has no conflict of interest. Purity is the outcome of continual exposure to God's presence. A stream is purest near its source. That is why the more time we spend in pri-vate devotion with the Lord Jesus, the more our motives, behav-iors and lifestyles begin to be more like Him. We are living near the source: Jesus.

Purity flourishes in the Inner Court as we commune with Jesus. There, we develop purity by confessing known sin, walk-ing in the light with others and lingering intimately with the Lord. Remember, our vision will change our character. The pure, single-minded heart sees God. If our eyes are on Jesus, our char-acter conforms to His image. If our eyes are on the things of this world, our character conforms to the world's image.

Jesus said, "The light of the body is the eye: if therefore thine eye be single, thy whole body shall be full of light" (Matt. 6:22, KJV). The believer who enters God's courts with a pure heart—going to be with Him rather than to get from Him—will be the darling of God's heart. The Lord makes us pure by His grace, but we have to look after the soul and body. We must submit to the Lord to become pure in spirit. When our souls (that is the mind, will and emotions) defile our prayer lives, spiritual discernment is immediately lost.

We who enter into the Holy Place must refuse to lift up our souls to materialistic idolatry or false ideas about God. We can-not be motivated by fleshly desires and expect to stand in His presence. "For God did not call us to be impure, but to live a holy life" (1 Thess. 4:7). The purity God requires from us is impossible for us. We must allow Him to produce it in us. Purity produces in us godliness when we consistently sit at the feet of Jesus.

## INTIMACY: KNOWING THE ONE
## WHO KNOWS US BEST

The more time we sit at His feet, the more intimately we will know Him. And the more we know Him, the more we will feel loved, secure and confident. "He has taken me to the banquet hall, and his banner over me is love" (Song of Songs 2:4).

Intimacy means "a very personal and private relationship characterizing one's deepest trust and nature marked by close association, contact and familiarity." Intimacy is not approached with a sense of duty; it is a love relationship between you and your heavenly Lover. To teach the art of loving is difficult. The language of love is strange and unnatural to the one who does not love! But it is perfectly natural to the lover!

Intimacy transcends the rational mind. Our desire for intimacy depends upon the state of the heart. As your heart is, so are you before the Lord. We can advance no further or deeper into the Holy Place of God's presence in intimate communion with Him, than we have allowed our hearts to be opened to and prepared for by the Spirit of God. The Scripture says, "As [a man] thinks in his heart, so is he" (Prov. 23:7, NKJV).

The mind gathers knowledge from God's Word and prepares the food by which the heart in the inner spirit is to be nourished. DANGER: Christians tend to believe that if they are occupied with the truth of the Word, spiritual intimacy will automatically result. This thinking is false. Our understanding deals with conceptions and images of divine things, but it cannot reach the real life of the inner spirit. Spiritual revelation can only come as we see, want, hunger and thirst. With the heart reaching out by faith and trust in our magnificent Lord, He fills the hungry and thirsty soul with spiritual impartation.

It is in our hearts (or spirit) that God has placed His Spirit, and He is there to build a bridge causing God's presence and power to work in us. Allow your spirit to linger in perfect humility and love.

Realize even now, in the hidden depths of your spirit that your heart is crying out for intimacy with your heavenly Bridegroom. Out of your innermost being you will want to know the deep things about your heavenly Father. As you become aware of God's good intention, you will gain the confidence to move closer to Him. Why is this so important? Because the effectiveness of your public ministry for God is dependent upon your intimacy with Him in the prayer closet.

As with any relationship, three primary steps must occur before real intimacy can be cultivated. Let's consider them.

## Step One: Acquaintance

An acquaintance is a person who knows Jesus but is not particularly close to Him. At salvation, we experience God's redeeming grace and His unconditional love, however, we do not automatically understand how to fellowship with Him. Jesus was disappointed that Philip needed further proof that He was the Son of God: "Jesus answered: 'Don't you know me, Philip, even after I have been among you such a long time?'" (John 14:9).

We cannot deeply love a person we slightly know. Yet, it is entirely possible to live with someone and not know him or her. Jesus was expressing this very problem. Perhaps you have been a Christian for many years and yet you do not have an intimate relationship with Jesus. The Christian life consists of much more than going to heaven when you die.

The first step toward greater intimacy starts with getting acquainted with your Savior. Quiet yourself before the Lord. Do not be talking or praying. Just sit in His presence. Allow your heart to be open to the Lord's touch. He wants to tell you how special you are to Him. He will not rebuke or punish a seeking heart. We serve a good God. He is aware of your hurts and fears. You can trust Him.

## Step Two: Friendship

Acquaintances that are maintained and cultivated eventually move to step two: friendships. The following story explains this transition succinctly:

> One day a happy Christian met an Irish peddler. He exclaimed, "It's a grand thing to be saved."
> "Ah," said the peddler, "it is, but I know something better than that."
> "Better than being saved?" said he.

"What can you possibly know better than that?"
"The friendship of the Man who has saved me!" was
the unexpected reply.[8]

Jesus said to His disciples, "I no longer call you servants, because a servant does not know his master's business. Instead, I have called you friends, for everything that I learned from my Father I have made known to you. You did not choose me, but I chose you and appointed you to go and bear fruit—fruit that will last" (John 15:15,16).

True friendship is rare, however, when it does occur, it bears the fruit of identity in thought, heart and spirit. As His disciples, we are to impart His heart to others. We may receive His blessings and quote His Word, but do we bear the fruit of friendship with Him?

The original Greek New Testament even had a special word for friendship-love: *philia*. That word, and the more familiar *agape*, often translate as "love" in our English Bibles. But the message conveyed in John 5:20 is that the Father is *close to* the Son.

### Step Three: Trust

Trust comes from trusting. For instance, when Bryan, our youngest son, was just a small boy, he asked his dad to put him on top of a large seven-foot-high concrete platform at the library. Eddie did so. After a few minutes, Eddie reached out his hands and said, "Jump, Bryan! Daddy will catch you."

Bryan was not so sure. Eddie said again, "Jump, son. I won't let you fall. You can trust me to catch you." Cautiously, but obediently, Bryan jumped into his daddy's arms.

About four months later, Bryan was climbing a tree at a park. When it was time to go, Eddie reached out his arms to Bryan and quietly said, "Jump." To Eddie's astonishment, Bryan joyfully jumped into the arms of his loving father. Trust had been developed by choosing to trust. Will you trust the Lord to hold you, to love you or to heal you? Will you jump into His loving arms? You can trust Him. He will not let you fall. "Those who trust in the Lord are like Mount Zion, which cannot be shaken but endures forever" (Ps. 125:1).

Most of the disappointment and pain we have suffered have

come from misplaced trust. We have loved God and trusted people. Some of those people have violated our trust. Now we must learn to trust God and love people!

## GROWING IN INTIMACY: AN
## ENCOUNTER WITH REAL LOVE

Many believers live or have lived in dysfunctional homes. It should not be surprising that the subject of intimacy is difficult for some to understand. Before God was ever the Creator, Judge, Lawgiver or Savior, He was a Father. A loving Father has the best in mind for the children He loves. I am finding that many in the Body of Christ doubt the Father's love. Three main reasons cause a reluctance for developing intimacy with God:

- Past hurts;
- A poor father figure;
- Refusing to deal with personal sin.

Notice, however, that these three reasons can be overcome by dealing with the past and deciding for the present. Please don't become trapped in the "victimization theology" within the Church today that says, "No wonder you cannot live in victory; just consider all you've been through." You can move from being what you were to who He wants you to be by allowing Him to re-Father you and re-fashion you into the likeness of His Son.

You may have lived through some terrible experiences, but you shouldn't wallow in them forever! If we are Christians, we are "new creations! Old things are to pass away! All things are to become new!" (see 2 Cor. 5:17).

As our friend evangelist Bobby Conner says, "Get over it!" He has given us "everything we need for life and godliness through our knowledge of him who called us by his own glory and goodness" (2 Pet. 1:3).

Because God is love, and He is the lover of your soul, who can better transform you into a lover than He?

"Years ago a sacred painting exhibited in a provincial town represented Christ upon the cross—not pain-racked and dying with eyes closed and face marred—but with eyes of infinite love looking out at the beholder. The room in which the picture was housed was dark and the painting was lighted from below. While a group of people were gathered to look at it, an intense hush fell upon the crowd. Forgetting his surroundings, a man standing in the front row who had become deeply absorbed in the painting whispered to himself, 'Jesus, I love you.'

"A man standing at his side, hearing the whisper and deeply moved, said, 'Yes, I love Him too.'

"Swiftly the words passed from lip to lip, till every heart was stirred by a warm passion for the Lord."[9] These people had an encounter with the reality of His love, which begins and ends with Him. "We love because he first loved us (1 John 4:19).

## UNVEILING THE TRUTH ABOUT YOU

1. Why does God need to develop your character before He recruits you into the battle of intercession?
2. Of the characteristics listed in this chapter, which do you possess? Which do you lack? What action will you take to create change?
3. Are you afraid to have an intimate relationship with Jesus Christ? What are the hurts, fears or stumbling blocks that separate you from Him?
4. As you consider the steps to intimacy, where are you in the process? Are you satisfied with where you are? If not, why?

### Notes

1. Milburn H. Miller, Notes and Quotes (Anderson, Ind: The Warner Press, 1960), p. 95.
2. Ibid., p. 180.
3. Paul E. Holdcraft, "Compassion on the World," Cyclopedia of Bible Illustrations (New York: Abingdon-Cokesbury Press, 1957), p. 279.
4. George Otis, Jr., The Last of the Giants (Tarryton, N.Y.: Chosen Books, 1991), p. 157.
5. Ibid., p. 157-158.
6. Oswald Chambers, My Utmost for His Highest (New York: Dodd, Mead & Company, 1935), p. 36.

7. *Cyclopedia of Bible Illustrations*, p. 142.
8. Rev. G.B.F. Hallock, *Best Modern Illustrations* (New York & London: Harper and Brothers Publishing Company, 1935), p. 80.
9. Ibid., p. 55.

# CHAPTER SEVEN

# The Journey Toward Intimacy

## IDENTIFIED IN DEATH

A lady once showed the famous artist Ruskin a costly handkerchief on which a blot of ink had been dropped. The handkerchief, she complained, was ruined. Nothing was left but to throw it away. Ruskin said nothing, but took the handkerchief away from her. Shortly afterward the lady received it back, but so changed that she could hardly believe it was the original. Using the ink blot as the basis, he had worked around it a beautiful and artistic design, changing what was valueless into a thing of beauty and joy."[1]

So it is with Christ. He takes the blots and failures of our lives and transforms them into valuable assets. Those hurts, disappointments and failures that appear to us as obstacles and threaten to ruin us become perfect opportunities for the Son of God to make new, if only we will let Him.

## UNDERSTANDING GOD'S WAY

Why does He allow us to experience this kind of pain? All life is the result of some form of brokenness. The earth must be broken before the seed can be planted. The seed must be broken before the plant can grow. And the earth must once again be broken before new plant life can emerge upon it. Brokenness then is a life-birthing process that must precede every area of growth in our lives. This is especially true as God develops our spiritual lives. Any spiritual fruitfulness will require the breaking of the outer person so the spirit can commune with the Spirit of Christ in us.

Prayer is the key! As we collapse into the arms of God, the outer person sloughs off like grave clothes. In prayer we see:

- The absolute holiness of God (see Rev. 15:4);
- Taste the joy of heaven (see John 16:7);
- Understand the reality of His Word (see Ps. 119:103).

Recognizing how Christ works in our lives is vitally important. Unless we understand the process, the journey can be quite discouraging. As a matter of fact, if we fail to understand the process, at the point where the Lord Jesus wants to draw us into a deeper experience with Himself, we will struggle against the journey toward intimacy, not realizing that we are actually being freed from the domination of our souls. We are being delivered daily from our carnal minds, our self-determined wills and the earthly emotions that enslave us. When we realize how very much unlike Jesus we are, our spirit cries out for His overcoming power.

We can experience this overcoming power if we are willing to yield to Him. Our human nature, however, resists surrendering to the will of another. And because of our stubborn, carnal love for self, the Father must break us so we may follow Jesus' example of becoming "broken bread" and "poured out wine" for His sake (see 1 Cor. 11:23-27). Broken bread is needful for life-giving service and poured out wine is needful to bring comfort to those who are hurting and perishing. Notice that the bread must be broken and the wine must be poured out.

As we reach the end of soul strength and begin to surrender to the process of spiritual maturity, we experience a freedom, a peace and a power yet unknown to us. This process can take a few years, even a lifetime. The stages of this spiritual journey usually occur gradually and are often a combination of many crises.

The dynamics of being drawn into intimacy are much like those of a midwife during the birth process. When the crisis heightens by nature's demands, the breaking of the water bag reassures us that one phase of life is ending to produce greater life. God's promise is that out of what has been broken will come greater life if we do not abort His process. Though it is difficult to

*The heavenly Bridegroom is wooing His Bride by destroying all her other lovers, with self being the biggest of all.*

understand why we need such agony, God provides the inner strength needed to take us through the labor to complete the work.

In every stage of our spiritual growth, new opportunities can strip away our soul's domination. The primary way of dealing with the "soul man" (commonly called flesh) is to deny it. We deny it any authority in our lives. The soul tries to rationalize, reason, figure and conclude what God is doing. But the Christian life is not to be a life of reasoning; it is to be a life of faith. And because it is a faith walk, any attempt to exercise willpower against the plan of God will only bring frustration.

Seeking the opinions of others will often delay the Spirit's work, as well. The heavenly Bridegroom is wooing His Bride by destroying all her other lovers, with self being the biggest of all.

God's plan begins as we elect to die to ourselves so the Lord can bring resurrection. I am not referring to the "new birth" of salvation. I am describing a metamorphosis in the life of a believer that precedes Christ's life flowing freely through that person.

Psalm 42:8 says, "By day the Lord directs his love, at night his song is with me—a prayer to the God of my life." Nothing can disturb the peace or lessen the passion that is present in the person who is walking in resurrection life because resurrection life produces the fruit of deepest love and intimacy with the Lord.

Antoine De Saint-Exupery once said, "Love does not consist

in gazing at each other, but in looking outward together in the same direction."[2]

## SOULISH APPROACHES TO GOD

If only believers would gaze upward instead of inward, we would understand God's way and we would not seek intimacy with Him in our own soulish ways. However, God says, "As the heavens are higher than the earth, so are my ways higher than your ways and my thoughts than your thoughts" (Isa. 55:9). The following are three ways that we believers often approach God:

1. Volitionally;
2. Emotionally;
3. Intellectually.

In each case (which we will cover in-depth later in this chapter), we are seeking to enter His presence in our grave clothes. The grave clothes are a metaphor for the flesh or soul—mind, will and emotions. But resurrection life can only fellowship with resurrection life! (See John 4:23,24.)

On the day of Jesus' resurrection, He left His grave clothes in the tomb. When Jesus raised Lazarus from the dead, His command was, "Loose him, and let him go" (John 11:44, *NKJV*). Many of us are bound by worldly attitudes and actions that entomb us. The stench of our dead works and self-promoting talk prevents us from seeing the truth about ourselves and God. We, too, need to strip off the remnant of our old unregenerate selves before we can begin to experience true intimacy with Christ. This is how it works...

"Jesus loved Martha and her sister [Mary] and [their brother] Lazarus" (John 11:5). Nevertheless, He did not hurry to the tomb. His job was to *resurrect* Lazarus, not heal him (see John 11:11). God is not interested in keeping our soulish selves in repair. He is wanting to "pronounce us dead." After all, He signed our death certificates with His own blood 2,000 years ago! (See Rom. 6:6.) The best statement we could hear about ourselves today would be what Lazarus could not hear about himself: "Then said

Jesus unto them plainly, 'Lazarus is dead'" (John 11:14, *NKJV*). The next verse says it all! "Jesus said, 'I am glad...let us go unto him'" (John 11:15, *NKJV*). Jesus knows firsthand that death must precede resurrection! (See Gal. 2:20.)

## THE VOLITIONAL APPROACH

Death will cause us to abandon the three primary soulish approaches to knowing God—the first of which is the volitional or performance approach. People who value performance think that what they *do* for God determines how much He loves them and how much He should do for them. Caught in the trap of performing, they view their productivity as an appraisal of their relationship with God. Driven by performance, they become legalistic and impatient with others who are not performance oriented.

They not only judge others by their own chosen personal disciplines, but they judge themselves to the point that they often suffer from discouragement and restlessness. These believers invent plans for God and rush forward to tackle any project with the greatest of zeal. But because they are constantly striving and driven, their souls are never quiet and rested. They have *no peace* and cannot *know peace* because their internal taskmaster gives them no time off for their good-works behavior. They become so driven by their internal perfectionist slave masters that they can be quite judgmental, frustrated, defeated and angry—especially and often unknowingly with God.

Their spiritual lives with God find them imprisoned and restricted. So the Lord allows many disappointments to come their way. Their emotions are often rigid and controlled, offering little spiritual sympathy for the pain of others. Spirit life cannot come forth because they are guarding their hearts. They may want to express compassion, but their outer man is in such control that they are unable to do so.

To reach the works-driven believer, God creates a crisis. He begins breaking their volitional wills through physical affliction, loss of job or other uncontrollable events. Still fearing failure and resisting God's brokenness, they seek to get affirmation from others by working harder. This actually delays the process of death to self. God will reveal their plight to them, for God alone can strip the soul.

Once brokenness has begun, the judgmental voice of self is gradually replaced with sensitivity to the loving, leading voice of the Holy Spirit. As the Spirit speaks into their hearts, they become aware of His presence and experience a desire to obey. This does not mean they become idle, but in time their activities become divinely directed and seasoned with supernatural love. As God crushes self, He replaces all soulish activity with Himself. Rather than being driven, these people can find peace in being led by the Holy Spirit.

This personality type can advance toward intimacy by learning to seek God with the same intensity used to seek the affirmation of people. They must practice the art of quietly meditating on the majesty of God. This will take effort, because in the past the outer man was in control. Altering their beliefs about who and what God is like is an essential part of their restorative process.

A biblical example of the performance personality is Martha who "had a sister called Mary, who sat at the Lord's feet listening to what he said. But Martha was distracted by all the preparations that had to be made. She came to him and asked, 'Lord, don't you care that my sister has left me to do the work by myself? Tell her to help me!'

"'Martha, Martha,' the Lord answered, 'you are worried and upset about many things, but only one thing is needed. Mary has chosen what is better, and it will not be taken away from her'" (Luke 10:39-42).

Oh, that those Marthas who are internally driven by a need to do more for God could understand the transforming power awaiting them in a life that is energized and motivated as it rests at the feet of Jesus and finds its strength from an overflow of His love within! This is what Michael de Molinos, the Spanish saint, taught in *The Spiritual Guide*: God will guide the soul by the hand and lead it through the way of pure faith, and "causing the understanding to leave behind all considerations and reasoning He draws her forward....Thus He causes her by means of a simple and obscure knowledge of faith to aspire only to her Bridegroom upon the wings of love."[3]

## STEPS TOWARD INTIMACY

Approaching the heavenly Bridegroom on the wings of love will happen as we take the following steps:

**Step 1:** Sit quietly before the Lord. Learn to read aloud intimate passages of the Word of God. (See Pss. 46; 51; 119; Song of Songs.) Speak them slowly and with expression. Tell the Lord you love Him repeatedly throughout the day.

**Step 2:** Choose to maintain an attitude of gratitude. (See Pss. 95:2; 100:4; Phil. 4:6; Col. 4:2; 1 Pet. 1:8; Rev. 7:12.)

**Step 3:** Ask the Lord for direction during the day. Do not fill the day with busyness, but focus on loving people. Be attentive to the Holy Spirit, allowing Him to speak to your heart about specific assignments. Be sure to ask Him for confirmation until you can recognize the voice of God. (See Pss. 19:7; 52:7; Isa. 26:3; Heb. 7:19; Jas. 1:25,26; 1 John 4:18,19.)

## THE EMOTIONAL APPROACH

Not everyone struggles with performance in their approach to God. Some struggle with pity and overvalue emotion, believing their tears will move Him. Frankly, as important as emotions are, Scripture reveals that faith, more than tears, moves the heart of God. "And without faith it is impossible to please God" (Heb. 11:6).

Controlled by their emotions, some believers are easily excitable and easily depressed. Their emotional roller coasters take them to the highest highs and the lowest lows. Left unbroken by God they can become gossips and manipulators absorbed in self pity, depression, unhappiness, anger and moodiness. As someone has said, "They suffer from ingrown eyeballs!"

Unlike others who must fight to express their emotions, these people actually flaunt theirs. Tears can even become the power they use to impress or even to control others. The intercessors who have never yielded their emotions to Christ, have difficulty discerning between the Lord's burden and their own soulish emotions. The core of the problem is selfishness.

The Lord wants to develop an intimate, mature relationship with these emotionally-driven believers, but unless they die to self-pity and selfishness, continuous whining will fill their prayer closets, and their self-absorbed tears will blind them to the ministry of the Spirit and the needs of others. The Lord did not put us here so others would minister to us. Instead, we are to minister to others. Jesus modeled this for us:

> Just as the Son of Man did not come to be served, but to serve, and to give his life as a ransom for many (Matt. 20:28).

We are to express the same Spirit-life that Jesus expressed, and crucify our self-lives. This is well illustrated in the story of the two water buckets tied on opposite ends of the same rope.

Day after day they would go down for water. They worked in the same well and carried the same water the same distance. One bucket, however, was always happy while the other bucket was always sad. After years of frustration, the happy bucket challenged the sad bucket in the middle of the well, "Why are you always so sad?"

The sad water bucket whined, "Because, it seems no matter how full I come up, I always go down empty."

The happy water bucket replied, "Not me, I figure no matter how empty I go down, I always come up full."

As we see in the story of these two buckets, attitude is a matter of choice and focus. Just as Jesus "endured the cross, scorning its shame," an intercessor who becomes intimate with the King of kings will endure, not complain. "Consider him who endured such opposition from sinful men, so that you will not grow weary and lose heart. In your struggle against sin, you have not yet resisted to the point of shedding your blood" (Heb. 12:3,4). We who have not shed our blood for others have no right to whine or complain. And when we catch His vision, surely we should expect to have His like-minded heart for lost souls.

But we cannot have His vision if we have a divided heart. "If any of you lacks wisdom, he should ask God, who gives generously to all without finding fault, and it will be given to him. But when he asks, he must believe and not doubt, because he who doubts is like a wave of the sea, blown and tossed by the wind. That man should not think he will receive anything from the Lord;

he is a double-minded man, unstable in all he does" (Jas. 1:5-8). We cannot be sold into self and sold out for Christ at the same time.

The word "double-minded" in the Greek is *dipsuchos,* which comes from the root *dis,* meaning "two" and *psuche,* meaning "the soul." These Scriptures therefore refer to one who is "two-souled," or one who has a divided heart. A heart is divided when the spirit grasps for faith and the soul is clinging to unbelief. Randy Shankle, in his book *The Merismos,* agrees:

> If your heart is divided, you then have dual interests, dual desires and dual affections. When your heart is divided, you will negate the forces that will change your life and the lives of those around you. If you do not keep your heart, it will not come forth with the forces of life. Remember that to keep it means "to guard it or protect it." What are you guarding your heart against? You are guarding against whatever desires to enter it, because whatever flows in will divide it.[4]

King Saul was a man driven by his emotions and divided in his interests. First Samuel 14 tells how King Saul bound the men of Israel under a royal oath not to eat during the battle against the Philistines. In his own greed for vengeance against his enemies, his "men were faint" from exhaustion (v. 28). Later in the evening the king found out that his own son, Jonathan, who was in the woods, had not heard the oath and had eaten honey. Saul pronounced a death sentence on him! It was Saul's officers who saved Jonathan from the sword.

One chapter later (see 1 Sam. 15), Saul ordered the Israelites into battle against the Amalekites. Samuel, the prophet, gave clear instruction from God that they were to kill every man, woman, child and animal in the Amalekite tribe. However, King Saul, again driven by his soulish desires, disobeyed God by saving King Agag and the best of the animals. In his anger, Samuel reprimanded Saul and announced that God had torn the kingdom from him.

King Saul replied, "I have sinned. I violated the Lord's command and your instructions. I was afraid of the people and so I gave in to them" (1 Sam. 15:24). One minute King Saul was ready to kill his own son; the next he was ready to spare a heathen king. Saul's undisciplined, double-minded life cost him his kingdom.

## STEPS TOWARD INTIMACY

Fortunately, no matter how double-minded we have been in the past, God is willing to extend the grace and mercy needed to change. We can partner with Him in the process by embracing the following steps:

**Step 1:** Avoid introspection. Focus on God. Do not make impulsive decisions, but patiently wait for the Lord's instructions. Do not allow your emotions to rule your decisions. Wait, when possible, for additional confirmations. (See Ps. 18:32-35; Isa. 26:3; Phil. 3:12; Jas. 1:1.)

**Step 2:** Check your motives. Refuse to call attention to self. Refuse to use prayer as a lifeline for gossip. Refuse to have a critical spirit. (See Prov. 11:25; 1 Cor. 10:24; Eph. 4:29; Phil. 2:3.)

**Step 3:** Worship the Lord with abandonment. Pray Scripture aloud. Forget your needs and press into the Lord. As you read the Word, allow each word to penetrate your spirit. Read parts of the Bible that will help you to stand firm in the faith. Renounce a double-mind and ask God to help you be single-minded. (See Pss. 18:32-40; 55:17-23; 140:1-8; 144:1-9; Prov. 4:23; Rom. 2:23-29; Heb. 11; 1 Pet. 3:4.)

## THE INTELLECTUAL APPROACH

As we have already discovered, some people approach God through their performance or wills and some through their emotions. Now we will consider those who approach God by depending on the third part of the soul—the intellect or mind. These believers tend to lean on formulas and principles for every situation. When the soul is dominant and unbroken, these people are often intellectual, power driven, restricted, haughty, stoic, untouched, insecure and idealistic. With mental confidence, they insist upon logical explanations for spiritual realities.

Their inclination is to elevate knowledge over experience.

They often control conversations with what seems to them to be impressive wisdom, however, they are unable to hold back that which expresses their true nature. Sadly, they must reveal what they are. They say more than they hear because they are fascinated with their own intelligence, and the sound of their own voices. In truth, they are speaking from the soul, not from the spirit:

> A fool's mouth is his undoing, and his lips are a snare to his soul. Before his downfall a man's heart is proud, but humility comes before honor (Prov. 18:7,12).

To set the intellectually-dependent believer free, the Lord then must work a twofold plan. First, He must break down the outer man; second, divide it from the spirit. The first is done through the *discipline* of the Holy Spirit, while the second is accomplished through the *revelation* of the Spirit. During the dividing phase, the Word of God, being quick and powerful, separates the spirit and the soul:

> For the word of God is living and active. Sharper than any double-edged sword, it penetrates even to dividing soul and spirit, joints and marrow; it judges the thoughts and attitudes of the heart (Heb. 4:12).

The twofold plan will involve separating three soulish categories:

- Spiritual and *natural forces;*
- Spiritual and *natural abilities;* and
- Spiritual and *natural talents.*

In his book *The Release of the Spirit,* Watchman Nee interestingly delineates the need for God's Word in the dividing of the spirit and soul:

> What then does God's Word do for us? It penetrates and divides. It is sharper than any two-edged sword. Its sharpness is demonstrated in the "penetrating to the division of soul and spirit, both of joints and marrow."

Note the analogy here: the two-edged sword against joints and marrow, and the Word of God against soul and spirit. Joints and marrow are embedded deeply in the human body. To separate the joints is to cut across the bones; to divide the marrow is to crack the bones. The two-edged sword can work thus in our mystical body. Only two things are harder to be divided than the joints and marrow; the soul and spirit. No sword, however sharp, can divide them. Even so we are wholly unable to distinguish between what is soul and what is spirit. Yet the Scripture tells us how the Living Word can do the job, for it is sharper than any two-edged sword. God's Word is living, operative, and able to penetrate and divide."[5]

This dividing is more than intellectual. It is the Word that permeates, and the Spirit that reveals to us our true motives. Deliverance can only come by divine revelation of the real nature of things. True knowledge is to discover what is of ourselves (from the soul), and what is of the Lord (from the spirit). Once revealed to us, we can ask the Holy Spirit to empower us through brokenness to live a resurrected life.

Uzziah's life points to the necessity for differentiating what is of the soul from what is of the spirit. He was 16 years old when he became king of Judah. "He sought God during the days of Zechariah, who instructed him in the fear of God. As long as he sought the Lord, God gave him success" (2 Chron. 26:5).

Uzziah was successful. His credits would have filled a hall of fame. His army won every battle, and every kingdom knew of his splendid reputation. He built towers and waterways in Jerusalem. All his fields and animals flourished. He had 307,500 well-trained, finely dressed military men. Yet his indictment came in 2 Chronicles 26:16, "But after Uzziah became powerful, his pride led to his downfall." The king entered the temple to burn incense, and in his defiance against the priests of God, the Lord afflicted him with leprosy for the rest of his life. Indeed, his pride led to a fall.

Jessie Penn-Lewis, in her book *Life Out of Death*, explains:

A true "self-effacement" does not mean a state of unconsciousness, it means that you become more acutely conscious, both of things around you and, above all, of Christ Himself. The only way you could know that Paul was "crucified" was that there was an entire absence of the "I" motive in all his words and actions."[6]

## STEPS TOWARD INTIMACY

What is motivating you? Would you like to be "crucified" so that you will reflect Christ in all of your words and actions. Let's look together at the steps you will need to take.

**Step 1:** Sit quietly before the Lord. Ask the Lord to break, to divide, your outward man daily. (See Rom. 1:9, 8:4-8; John 4:23,24; 12:24; 1 Cor. 2:11-14; 2 Cor. 3:6.)

**Step 2:** Study the Scripture from a relational point of view. Tell the Lord how much you want a close relationship, instead of cognitive knowledge about Him. Read passionate verses aloud. Free your mind while in prayer, by keeping a pen and notebook handy to write down the thoughts that clutter your mind constantly. (See Pss. 63:3-11; 86; Phil. 2:1-7; 1 Tim. 6:7-11; Jas. 2:3-8; Rev. 12:11.)

**Step 3:** Be real. Refuse to hide behind the prideful walls of intelluctualism. Realize that love is more important to God than human reasoning. (See Mark 12:33; John 8:32,36; 1 Cor. 13; 1 Pet. 1.22; 3 John 1:4.)

## STRIPPING THE SOUL FOR
## AN ETERNAL GOAL

The Lord loves each one of us too much to leave us where we are. Therefore, once we say yes to His ways in our lives, He will dig up the hardened ground in our spiritual soil and remove the calluses from our hardened hearts by stripping the soul. Three primary tools are used to bring us to total surrender, and He alone selects the most effective and timely tools for our circumstances. In varying degrees He will use all three:

- Suffering;
- Brokenness;
- Failure.

## Suffering

One of the tools most effective for building godly character is suffering. And though every person will encounter some suffering in his or her lifetime, for the Christian suffering will eventually result in greater glory. "Now if we are children, then we are heirs—heirs of God and co-heirs with Christ, if indeed we share in his sufferings in order that we may also share in his glory" (Rom. 8:17).

Often, however, we fall prey to thinking that suffering will happen only once. But stripping the soul is a process that happens throughout a lifetime. Every stage of stripping the soulish life includes a beginning, a working out and a completion. The end of one stage is the entrance to the next. The process is the same in every stage. We are sometimes confused because it seems that in each stage the lessons are repetitive. In truth, we are continually learning at deeper degrees.

When a much stronger force of demonic opposition comes against us than we remember from the past, it is because we have moved into a deeper level with Christ through suffering. As author and speaker Francis Frangipane said, "new level, new devil." We must be willing, in the anointing of the Spirit, to move forward aggressively against the powers of darkness. As our spirit lives are strengthened, the Lord allows more trials. Yet we are able to bear them with our newly acquired level of spiritual power which is Christ's resurrected life in us. In this we become victorious overcomers!

We can say with David, "Thou hast enlarged me when I was in distress" (Ps. 4:1, *KJV*). The best news of all is that "To him who overcomes, I will give the right to sit with me on my throne, just as I overcame and sat down with my Father on his throne" (Rev. 3:21).

## Brokenness

Randy Shankle describes in his book *The Merismos*, "The key to releasing the spirit man is found in the word brokenness. What does brokenness do to a stony heart? It breaks it up. Jeremiah 4:3 says: 'Break up your unplowed ground and do not sow among thorns.' Fallow ground becomes hardened by exposure to the elements. If you allow your soul to be exposed to the elements [or world] for a long time and not to the things of Jesus, your soul man will harden over. It will become rough, rigid and nonresponsive to the touch of God."[7]

Jeremiah explained to the people that before God could bring forth life from them, He would have to bring brokenness to remove all soul strength. Once brokenness was complete, the spirit man could have preeminence.

In the spring of 1989, the Lord began dealing with me about taking a sabbatical from selling real estate. At the time I was a successful real estate agent in Houston, Texas. I had experienced a financially profitable year. In the fall of 1989, I went for a weekend to spend time with the Lord. I knew in my heart that He was

*Brokenness is not our enemy;*
*it is our friend.*

going to ask some difficult questions of me. As I lay praying on the floor of a hotel room, the Lord spoke to me with clarity such as I had never heard before.

He said, *Alice, will you give up your real estate business in 1990 to do nothing but minister to Me and pray?*

I could feel my body tighten as I groaned over my answer, *Lord, I love my work and I am so good at it.*

Sadly, I could feel a resistance that surprised even me. Again, as He repeated the words, waves of love seemed to roll over me. I cried bitterly to think that anything could possibly be more important to me than He. He revealed how I was finding my significance in my real estate success. Unsettled, I wept as never before.

Then with an indescribable love He gently said, *I gave everything for you, won't you give this to Me?* The dam of resistance inside of me broke and submission flooded my heart. Absolute surrender was my answer that evening. I spent the next two months closing down my real estate business. My assignment for 1990 was simple: PRAY! This is the way of consecration, and with John I say, "He must become greater; I must become less" (John 3:30).

I cannot tell you how grateful I am for the ongoing breaking process in my own life. I have come to realize that brokenness is not our enemy; it is our friend. God wants us to have "a broken spirit; a broken and contrite heart, O God, you will not despise" (Ps. 51:17). The definition of contrite is "to be humble or quick to repent." When brokenness occurs, resistance, independence and pride are replaced with submission, tenderness, obedience and love.

## Failure

Failure is an especially difficult issue for the twentieth-century western mind. From birth we are taught the importance of success. Whether it is the young person in the beauty pageant or the little boy in the peewee or T-ball league, the message is the same:

Winning is everything!

The necessity to win feeds our self-sufficiency. We find ourselves saying as the church in Laodicea, "I am rich; I have acquired wealth and do not need a thing" (Rev. 3:17). In other words, "I am a winner!" We are so accustomed to saying so, that we can even fake it if necessary. It is perhaps here that God meets His biggest challenge in stripping the soul. Here is where He must allow us to fail so completely and so miserably that we will never again seek sufficiency in self.

As Christ told the apostle Paul, "My grace is sufficient for you, for my power is made perfect in weakness" (2 Cor. 12:9). From this point on, we find our sufficiency in His grace! We can no longer boast of our victories. We can no longer brag about our successes. We no longer need to succeed. We are able to "boast all the more gladly about [our] weaknesses, so that Christ's power may rest on [us]" (2 Cor. 12:9).

It is a liberating feeling to no longer strive for success. No longer am I driven to win! Never again will human opinions manipulate me! No longer will I esteem myself and accept Him! Now I can accept myself and esteem Him!

## THE SUBMISSION OF THE SOUL

In order to come to the place where He is esteemed above self, we must actively submit. Active submission is different from passive acceptance. It is willful participation, even partnership with the Father in the process. What looks impossible when God starts the process, in time will produce a fresh sweetness within.

Few people have more clearly demonstrated a life so fully submitted to Christ as that of the Spaffords, a fine Christian family who lived in Chicago during the 1850s. Horatio (commonly referred to as H.G.) and Anna Spafford were pillars of the community, serving those in need. They were supporters of Dwight L. Moody and helped establish his ministry. In 1871 when the Chicago fire struck, the Spaffords worked faithfully to help the survivors in the aftermath of the fire.

By 1873 the stress of their many years of relief work finally took its toll on Anna Spafford. Doctors advised Anna to take a vacation. H.G. Spafford had visited France years before and decided this would be the perfect place to take his family. He booked the voyage for the family on the *Ville du Havre*, the safest and most luxurious ship afloat. With great anticipation, their four daughters along with their governess prepared for the voyage. As the date for their departure approached, a business problem prevented H.G. from sailing with the rest of the family. He promised, however, to join them on their vacation as soon as possible.

During the journey across the Atlantic Ocean, on a calm, starry night, the *Ville du Havre* was rammed midship. Despite reassurances from the crew, the ship split in two and sank within 15 minutes, taking the Spafford family to the ocean's depths. Anna Spafford felt her infant daughter slip from her arms as she sunk under the water by the force of the sea. Only by a miracle was Anna saved. A piece of wood planking had floated up under her unconscious body, bringing her to the surface. Only 57 people survived, including Anna and the governess. Gone were the Spafford's four precious daughters.

Upon arrival in France, Anna cabled Horatio with just two words, "Saved alone." In his grief-stricken state, H.G. quickly booked passage on another ship to meet his wife. While on the ship in recluse, the captain summoned Mr. Spafford to come to him in the wheel house. Peering into the starry night, the captain said, "Sir, this is where the *Ville du Havre* sank." After gazing into the watery grave of his four little daughters, Horatio wiped the tears from his eyes and retired to his cabin below. There he took a pen and paper and wrote:

> When peace, like a river,
> attendeth my way,
> When sorrows like sea billows roll,
> Whatever my lot, thou has taught me to know:
> It is well, it is well, with my soul.

Note: The original says, "thou has taught me to know," which has a much deeper meaning. The words expressed his continued faith in the face of complete disaster.

As you press forward with God from stage to stage, completing the warfare with your own soul and achieving victory on each level, you can then lead others through the same process. We can lead others no farther than we have gone ourselves.

Today we are beginning to understand our position as the Bride of Christ. To date, we have lived, at best, as a "girlfriend." In the next chapter we will look deeply into the significance of being His Bride.

### Unveiling the Truth About You

1. Why does the Lord want to strip your soul of self-interest? Have you misunderstood the process? Will you say yes to the process?
2. Can you identify with one of the soulish approaches to God? Which one? What must you do to draw closer to Him?
3. As you reflect on your life, where do you need to repent for fighting against God's will? Where do you presently need to surrender in order to draw closer to Him?

## Notes

1. Rev. G. B. F. Hallock, *Best Modern Illustrations* (New York: Harper and Brothers Publishers, 1935), illustration 2319, p. 364.
2. Michael de Molinos, *The Spiritual Guide* (Methune & Co., Ltd, sixth edition, 1950), p. 56.
3. Ibid., p. 69.
4. Randy Shankle, *The Merismos* (Tulsa, Okla.: Christian Publishing Services, Inc., 1987), p. 212.
5. Watchman Nee, *The Release of the Spirit* (Cloverdale, Ind.: Sure Foundation Publishers, 1965), pp. 68-69.
6. Jessie Penn-Lewis, *Life Out of Death* (Parkstone, England: Overcomer Publications, Preface to Revised Edition, 1900), p. 49.
7. Shankle, p. 218.

# CHAPTER EIGHT

# Romance of the Heart

## FROM COVENANT TO CONSUMMATION

This spring morning is unlike all others. Throughout the house the air is charged with excitement! This is the wedding day. The Bride stands gazing into the full-length mirror with a look of almost disbelief. She quickly comes to attention as she pivots around to tell everyone about her Groom with whom she is beginning a new life. She explains, "He is not just any man. He is a King, and He is not just any king, He is the King of kings!" She has letters from this stately King of all kings with promises of eternal things to come. With great joy, she prepares for the wedding.

### CHOSEN TO BE THE BRIDE

Inside her room the Bride takes the necessary time to beautify herself. Her gown is made of white flowing linen. From her perfumed neck hangs the gift of pearls given to her by Jesus, her Husband. They are symbolic of the great price He has paid for her. And now as the Bride gazes at her reflection in the mirror, joy floods her heart. JESUS, the Bridegroom, has chosen her, the CHURCH, "to present her to himself as a radiant church, without stain or wrinkle or any other blemish, but holy and blameless" (Eph. 5:27).

What is the scriptural significance of the Bride? What is to be our wedded relationship with Jesus? When is it to occur? Many believe it is a future event. They see the marriage as a future

Kingdom reality. I believe the marriage is now. I believe the marriage supper of the Lamb is not the wedding; it is more like an anniversary celebration. The wedding is the new birth; the marriage is the Christian life. Solomon's Song of Songs reveals much to us about this marriage. Let's look into the phases of this intimate spirit-to-Spirit relationship.

## THE HONEYMOON: GETTING TO KNOW HIM

Let him kiss me with the kisses of his mouth—for your love is more delightful than wine. Pleasing is the fragrance of your perfumes; your name is like perfume poured out. No wonder the maidens love you! Take me away with you—let us hurry! Let the king bring me into his chambers (Song of Songs 1:2-4).

When the inner spirit plunges into the fathomless ocean of God's love, consummation of a divine union has occurred. Male or female, all are one in Christ. The Bride and her heavenly Groom are one. This relationship is like a sweet perfume that fills the air. In the life of this new partnership, the human spirit experiences the joy of forgiveness, and the assurance of life eternal. An awakening of the inner life has occurred.

During the honeymoon phase of any new marriage, love is immature. As we see in this passage from Song of Songs, the Bride encourages her heavenly Lover to meet her needs. "Let Him kiss me." Her impatience can be heard in verse 4, "Take me away with you—let us hurry!" This desire for all her needs to be met should not be considered bad, only immature. The same is true when we begin our relationship with Jesus. We depend heavily on His reinforcing love. As the relationship deepens, however, we learn to give our love to Him more freely.

## AND HIS WAYS SHALL BECOME MY WAYS

We can *know* our heavenly Bridegroom Spirit to spirit. God longs to know us and to make Himself known to us. And once we *know*

Him, we must learn His ways. Sadly, some desire His benefits, but "they say unto God,...we desire not the knowledge of thy ways" (Job 21:14, *KJV*).

David, whom God called a man after His own heart, wrote, "Show me thy ways, O Lord" (Ps. 25:4, *KJV*). But God grieved over Israel because, though they knew Him, they never learned His ways (see Pss. 84:5; 95:10). The psalmist explained, "He made known his ways unto Moses, his acts unto the children of Israel" (Ps. 103:7, *KJV*). The Israelites knew what God did, but Moses knew why God did it. That is a deeper relationship!

We can be married to someone and never really know what or why that person does what he or she does. Until we fully understand a person's ways, we can't fully know the heart. King David understood this important union by writing, "Create in me a clean heart, O God; and renew a right spirit within me....Then will I teach transgressors thy ways; and sinners shall be converted unto thee" (Ps. 51:10,13, *KJV*). Only those who have learned God's ways can teach them to others! Only those who have known the deep joy of being fully married to Him can contagiously transmit that joy to others.

## BASKING IN THE BENEFITS

Why do you suppose that married people are usually trying to find a mate for their single friends? They know that we are all fashioned by our Creator for relational intimacy, and that intimacy is best seen between the Bride and her Groom. Let's look at some of the benefits.

### Companionship
One of the first benefits experienced in marriage is companionship. "He has taken me to the banquet hall, and his banner over me is love" (Song of Songs 2:4).

Those who have lost loved ones through death tell us the awful agony of being alone. Loneliness is a very painful reality, but the Lord did not create us to be alone. After creating Adam, rather than His usual pronouncement of, "It is good," God said, "It is not good that man should be alone." (Gen. 2:18, *KJV*). It was the Father's idea to create a woman for man. From the beginning, it was important to the Father that neither He, nor man, be alone.

## Sustenance

And not only is God concerned that we have companionship, but like any good husband, He sustains us:

> Like an apple tree among the trees of the forest is my lover among the young men. I delight to sit in his shade, and his fruit is sweet to my taste....Strengthen me with raisins, refresh me with apples, for I am faint with love" (Song of Songs 2:3,5).

The Lord Jesus feeds us by speaking to us. He also feeds us with the Word of God. He encourages us to "Taste and see that the Lord is good" (Ps. 34:8). As we feed on the Word, we take hold of it. As we apply it in our daily lives, it takes hold of us!

The book of Ruth clearly portrays the sustenance of the heavenly marital relationship. When both Naomi and her Moabite daughter-in-law, Ruth, became widowed, both were without food or provision. Traveling from Moab to Bethlehem, Ruth committed to stay with Naomi. When they arrived in Bethlehem, God granted Ruth favor as she gleaned behind the harvesters in the fields of Boaz, her father-in-law's next of kin. Day after day, Ruth gleaned more than enough grain for Naomi and herself. When Naomi instructed Ruth to lay at the feet of Boaz during the night, asking Boaz to spread his skirt over her, a symbol of taking her under his protection by marriage, this sign of humility and surrender touched the heart of Boaz. Boaz, in return, went to the city gate and redeemed the field of Naomi's late husband, Elimelech. Upon buying the field in the presence of the city elders, Boaz fulfills the law of a kinsman-redeemer by announcing:

> Today you are witnesses that I have bought from Naomi all the property of Elimelech, Kilion and Mahlon. I have also acquired Ruth the Moabitess, Mahlon's widow, as my wife, in order to maintain the name of the dead with his property, so that his name will not disappear from

among his family or from the town records. Today you
are witnesses! (Ruth 4:9,10).

Boaz took Ruth to be his wife. Everything that belonged to
Boaz now belonged to Ruth. From their relationship came Obed,
the grandfather of King David. And through that line we, too,
have reaped a Husband and a King.

## Affection

Like any loving husband, the Lord shows us His affection. "His
left arm is under my head, and His right arm embraces me"
(Song of Songs 2:6). As we enter marriage, the inward fountain of

*We have "gleaned in the fields" so long that we feel unworthy to sit beside Him at the banquet table.*

love increases. The heavenly Bridegroom wants to express His
unconditional love for us. One difficulty we encounter is trying
to measure up to this undeserved favor. We have "gleaned in the
fields" so long that we feel unworthy to sit beside Him at the
banquet table. Not until we quiet our minds from the restless
expectations of what we think He wants from us can we enjoy
His favorable affection. As Outer Court striving ends and we
become aware of our acceptance in Christ, an inward rest allows
us to receive the genuine affection of the Bridegroom.

In absolutely no way is this meant to be a sexual affection. I
am referring to the affection we experience when our hearts have
been touched by a love that transcends anything this world could
offer.

## Protection

A byproduct of His love and affection is the security of His protection. "But you are a shield around me....I lie down and sleep; I wake again, because the Lord sustains me....I will not fear the tens of thousands drawn up against me on every side....From the Lord comes deliverance" (Ps. 3:3-8). If we would experience a deeper relationship with Jesus Christ, we must learn to hide in the shadow of His wing. Just as Ruth asked Boaz to spread his skirt over her, our heavenly Groom longs to spread His skirt over us to offer protection. His banner over us is love!

As we daily abide in Him, then what comes to us is by His permission. We learn as Paul did that "in whatsoever state I am, therewith to be content" (Phil. 4:11, *KJV*), and as did Timothy that "godliness with contentment is great gain" (1 Tim. 6:6). Therefore, as we develop perfect confidence in His protection, the relationship is deepened in trust and fruitful in faithfulness.

## DEVELOPING YOUR ETERNAL MARRIAGE

Our marriage with Christ develops as we cultivate fellowship, Bible study, fasting, meditation, witnessing, service, prayer and other faithful acts of giving and receiving. Unfortunately, intimate prayer is the most often overlooked.

As we experience prolonged intimate prayer, He produces growth and fruitfulness in our lives. Time in His presence causes us to become so satisfied and refreshed that all other loves pale in comparison.

> Listen! My lover! Look! Here he comes, leaping across the mountains, bounding over the hills. My lover is like a gazelle or a young stag. Look! There he stands behind our wall, gazing through the windows, peering through the lattice. My lover spoke and said to me, "Arise, my darling, my beautiful one, and come with me. See! The winter is past; the rains are over and gone. Flowers appear on the earth; the season of singing has come, the cooing of doves is heard in our land. The fig tree forms its early fruit; the blossoming vines spread their fragrance. Arise, come, my darling; my beautiful one, come with me" (Song of Songs 2:8-13).

His words drip with love and grace for His Bride and through them the Bride is forever changed. This change results in fruitfulness. The fragrance of flowers follow her everywhere, a song lingers on her lips and the sweet presence of a dove is heard cooing in delight of this union. Knowing her heavenly Bridegroom and what is important to Him becomes more important to her as she gets to know Him. She learns that once limited with Him through the new birth, she must now abandon herself to Him by spending time with Him, reading His Word and listening to His voice. And the more she does, the more her heart cries out for an even greater revelation of who He is.

## THE REVELATION

Of all the things He reveals to us, nothing is more precious, nothing is more relational than the revelation of Himself. He is under no obligation to share Himself with us, but He does. As our heav-

*He has rent the veil, but we must open the door! We must risk being known completely if we are to be complete in Him.*

enly Lover reveals the hidden secrets of His heart, we are deeply affected. Having our senses deadened daily to the "self-life" (Rom. 6:11), our spirit is magnetically drawn into the vast ocean of His love.

Amazingly, God invites us to Himself. "My lover spoke and said to me, 'Arise, my darling, my beautiful one, and come with me'" (Song of Songs 2:10). We have a choice. We can stay in the Outer Court of inferiority or we can voluntarily turn our minds, wills, and emotions toward the Spirit and draw closer to Him. He has rent the veil, but we must open the door! We must risk being known completely if we are to be complete in Him.

## TESTING THE RELATIONSHIP

And how will we be made complete? It will happen as our love is refined. Our instruction is to "buy from me gold refined in the fire" (Rev. 3:18). James calls this the "the testing of your faith [which] develops perseverance" (Jas 1:3).

This testing is the most intriguing part of God's plan. It is one of "His ways." Moses knew the ways of God because he prayed, "If you [Lord] are pleased with me, teach me your ways so I may know you and continue to find favor with you. Remember that this nation is your people" (Exod. 33:13). But Christians today often view God's testing as rejection. On the contrary.

One of the ways He tests our relationship is by withholding Himself from us. He withdraws:

> My dove in the clefts of the rock, in the hiding places on the mountainside, show me your face, let me hear your voice; for your voice is sweet, and your face is lovely....I opened for my lover, but my lover had left; he was gone. My heart sank at his departure. I looked for him but did not find him. I called him but he did not answer. The watchmen found me as they made their rounds in the city. They beat me, they bruised me; they took away my cloak, those watchmen of the walls! O daughters of Jerusalem, I charge you—if you find my lover, what will you tell him? Tell him I am faint with love (Song of Songs 2:14; 5:6-8).

When God withdraws, it is only to teach us the importance of walking daily with Him. Permit me to explain as I share a childhood story about my husband, Eddie. As a very young boy, Eddie enjoyed going to Woolworth's department store in downtown Birmingham, Alabama, with his grandmother. I am told that he would jerk loose from her hand the moment they entered the store and barrel straight into the toy department.

On one of their visits, Eddie made his usual dash toward the toys only to discover that the toy department had moved. Suddenly he was less interested in toys and more interested in finding his grandmother. He scoured the store, crying out to her.

Years later, she confessed that as Eddie came down one aisle looking for her, she would hide quietly from him behind a display until he had passed. When she finally did show herself to him, Eddie ran and grabbed her with such force that she wondered if he would have to be surgically removed! Why did she hide from him? Certainly not because she didn't love him. She treasured him. She hid from him to teach him how to walk with her!

Our heavenly Groom pulls away for a season so the Bride can experience the loss of His manifested presence. He takes away the spiritual riches (His gifts) bestowed on us as newlyweds. Often, He also temporarily withdraws His voice and the anointing for service. It's difficult to understand why He withdraws from us at all. And during these withdrawal seasons, the absence of His expressed presence produces a dryness of soul:

You are a garden locked up, my sister, my bride; you are
a spring enclosed, a sealed fountain (Song of Songs 4:12).

Notice the use of the word "my" in this passage. We are His Bride, and He will go to any length to have His Bride to Himself. The words "spring enclosed, a sealed fountain" suggest that the Bride had become frigid. The fountain of love and adoration that had once poured out of her had ceased to flow. Is your love for the heavenly Bridegroom cold? Has He withdrawn from you? Have you ceased to pursue Him?

I remember the devotion of your youth, how as a bride
you loved me and followed me through the desert,
through a land not sown (Jer. 2:2).

He longs to be pursued. God refuses to be taken for granted. So by being silent, or withholding His anointing from our lives, He "creates a crisis" in our hearts. This, in turn, creates a hunger and thirst for Him within our spirit.

Awake, north wind, and come, south wind! (Song of Songs 4:16).

It is as though the Bride experiences temporary death. The Lord removes all conscious experience of His grace and love. The soul is tormented by this death (wilderness experience) and struggles to find God even if it means serving in the flesh to do so. When this fails (as it will), the Bride realizes how she has taken her Groom for granted. Out of this grief and repentance come tears of godly sorrow. Her surrender draws the heavenly Bridegroom again to her with new tokens of His love.

The Bride hardly recovers before she again forgets her Lover is Jesus. The spirit wants what is of God, while the soul wants what is of self. The Lord grieves as He realizes the Bride is so unfaithful. "Does a maiden forget her jewelry, a bride her wedding ornaments? Yet my people have forgotten me, days without number" (Jer. 2:32). She sinks into a desperation until which time the spirit man takes preeminence. This cycle continues until the Bride learns to abide in complete surrender to her Groom.

Waiting in anticipation for His abiding presence encourages the pursuit. Passionate pursuit balanced with patience in the process yields a harvest of godly discipline. Such patience is a bit easier when we begin to know the process and the Father's ways. In the plan of God, the process is the end. Our journey, as the Bride, is to stay in continual pursuit of our Lover.

All night long on my bed I looked for the one my heart loves; I looked for him but did not find him. I will get up now and go about the city, through its streets and squares; I will search for the one my heart loves. So I looked for him but did not find him (Song of Songs 3:1,2).

Having begun to learn His ways during the periods of dryness, self-examination inevitably arises. But we should not allow this introspection to be reduced to self-condemnation (see Rom. 8:1). Godly self-evaluation will expose hidden sins and selfish motives that spoil our relationship with Him. Self-examination is for the purpose of purifying our love.

> Catch for us the foxes, the little foxes that ruin the vine-
> yards, our vineyards that are in bloom (Song of Songs
> 2:15).

The "little foxes" are subtle sins that creep into our lives and seek to rob us of relationship. Sins not only deprive us of intimacy, but they also deprive us of love. As we rid ourselves of them, we cleanse ourselves for Him.

In the beginning of the relationship, He showered us with gifts as tokens of His love. Now the time to temporarily remove them comes, so an unhealthy root of self-dependency cannot form. You may ask, "If the gifts are so harmful, why does He bother giving them at all?" Our heavenly Lover gives gifts to draw the Bride to Himself. As we start exercising and enjoying these spiritual gifts, a dangerous admiration of self tends to arise. Along with a growing admiration for our spiritual victories, a self-righteous confidence begins to take root in us. Then just as we begin to think we are something so special that we don't really need Him, the Lord withdraws His blessings. He temporarily withholds many spiritual gifts, so we can see a fuller revelation of how bankrupt we really are apart from Him. This bankruptcy reminds us that we cannot live Christian lives under self-rule.

## RENEWAL: THE SPRINGTIME OF OUR LOVE

A rekindled assurance of God's work is right on time. The winter season has now passed. Promise of spring is coming! Out of her spirit, the Bride knows by experiential revelation that she is married to the Lord. Those areas of her life where thoughts, imaginations, intellect and emotions once governed are now beginning to submit to the Spirit of God within her.

> How beautiful you are and how pleasing, O love, with
> your delights! Your stature is like that of the palm, and
> your breasts like clusters of fruit...the clusters of the
> vine, the fragrance of your breath like apples, and your
> mouth like the best wine....Let us go early to the vine-
> yards to see if the vines have budded, if their blossoms
> have opened, and if the pomegranates are in bloom—

there I will give you my love. The mandrakes send out
their fragrance, and at our door is every delicacy, both
new and old, that I have stored up for you, my lover
(Song of Songs 7:6-13).

Strangely, He doesn't come expressing who He is to her, but
rather who she is to Him. As in many things of the Spirit, many
of us have assumed the opposite. We think our relationship is
largely built on who He is to us, when in fact, before He was anything to us, we were specially loved by Him. "But God demon-
strates his own love for us in this: While we were still sinners,
Christ died for us" (Rom. 5:8).

Most of us are far more ready to believe how much we
should love God than we are to believe how much He loves us.
Perhaps that is because one who loves as much as He loves us
has great responsibility. The "old" in Song of Songs 7:13 (which
we just read) might be His age-old promises (see 2 Pet. 1:4).
However, just having the promises is insufficient. The "new" is
our *experience* with those "very great and precious promises."
Love is not really love until it has been backed up with action.

All that has taken place up to this point has been immature
love (or selfishness), but now the Bride's love is becoming selfless.
"I belong to my lover, and his desire is for me" (Song of Songs
7:10). She *responds* to Him. She finally finds faith enough to *believe*
what He says she is to Him. The Bridegroom has established the
courtship protocol; seek and find. The fact that the Bride begins
this pursuit tells us that she is committed to finding mature love.
In chapter 8, verse 1, she says, "If only you were to me like a
brother, who was nursed at my mother's breasts! Then, if I found
you outside, I would kiss you, and no one would despise me." By
this she lets us know that her love for Him as her Lord and King
is like the feeling for a brother, pure and simple love.

Few Christians really understand and feel that they are a
delight to the Lord. Because they misunderstand the courtship of
heaven, they misinterpret His silence as abandonment or rejection. Uniquely, it is the revelation that we are a delight to God
that enables us to move boldly into the throne room. With a
supernatural assurance of love, now the Bride becomes what He
needs:

I am a wall, and my breasts are like towers. Thus I have become in his eyes like one bringing contentment (Song of Songs 8:10).

In no way am I implying that this physical metaphor is sexual. It refers to the place where the Bride brings comfort and gives love. Lifted out of the selfish mind-set, the Bride finds a boundless capacity to love God from the depths of her spirit. The Bride now enters the life that springs forth from death, a life with the heavenly Bridegroom. Her sole joy is to bring contentment to her Spiritual Lover. The Lord finds comfort in her faithful, strong and mature companionship.

Does God have needs? In one sense He does not, yet in another sense (because of His self-limitation) He does. In the sense that He looks for people to stand in the gap, and for those who worship Him in Spirit and in truth, He has chosen to "need" a relationship with us. He also equips us to fulfill His expectations within that relationship.

## A PASSION FOR PARTNERSHIP

Inherent in our relationship with God is a partnership that has a desired, achievable and fruitful end.

First, God wants us to partner with Him in filling the earth not only with His glory, but also with "the knowledge of the glory of the Lord" (Hab. 2:14, *KJV*). He has covenanted to do this by filling the earth with sons and daughters. You see, God has never stopped making humans "in His own image" (Gen. 1:27). He is conforming all who will relate to Him into the image of His Son (Rom. 8:29).

Second, He will achieve His goals through His relationship with us. Because He refers to us as His Bride, at the new birth we became one spirit with Him just as a man becomes one flesh with a wife. The wife's natural desire is for her husband, and from this healthy relationship, intimate love develops.

Passion transforms into trust and trust into deep abiding companionship. Companionship leads to abandonment, and abandonment results in sacrificial love. Abandoned and faithful lovers will lay down their lives for each other. This is the kind of love Christ is looking for today:

> Place me like a seal over your heart, like a seal on your arm; for love is as strong as death, its jealousy unyielding as the grave. It burns like blazing fire, like a mighty flame. Many waters cannot quench love; rivers cannot wash it away. If one were to give all the wealth of his house for love, it would be utterly scorned (Song of Songs 8:6,7).

Third, the Father has chosen to call this a marriage relationship. We are a Bride given to Jesus. He is a Husband given to us. "For your Maker is your husband—the Lord Almighty is his name—the Holy One of Israel is your Redeemer; he is called the God of all the earth" (Isa. 54:5). Since the beginning of time the Father has been interested in family relationship and fellowship.

Finally, this is a relationship with an expected result. He not only wants us to experience intimacy with Him, but He also longs for that intimacy to result in a conception which will produce fruit that remains (see John 15:8).

Jesus Christ wants His Bride to be pregnant with His burden for the 2.5 billion boys, girls, men and women who have never heard the love story of Calvary. Our God is thrilled that you and I are part of His family, but He still weeps for the many others who have not received His Spirit of adoption. The Bride must seek the bed chamber (prayer closet) where this burden can be imparted. She must long to be spiritually intimate with her heavenly Bridegroom.

It disappoints the Lord that His Bride does not want to conceive His spiritual seed in her heart. The chilling truth is that the Church has many other lovers: cars, careers, houses, entertainment, money and fame. "'She has gone up on every high hill and under every spreading tree and has committed adultery there....You have lived as a prostitute with many lovers—would you now return to me?' declares the Lord" (Jer. 3:6,1).

Many who conceive are not willing to carry the burden to full term. Instead they abort His seed. The Bride's labor of love requires a death to self that she must choose and He must administer. "I tell you the truth," Jesus said, "unless a kernel of wheat falls to the ground and dies, it remains only a single seed. But if it dies, it produces many seeds. The man who loves his life will lose it, while the man who hates his life in this world will keep it for eternal life" (John 12:24,25).

## GIVING BIRTH TO WIND

Isaiah 26:17,18 states the condition of the Church in many parts of the world:

> As a woman with child and about to give birth writhes and cries out in her pain, so were we in your presence, O Lord. We were with child, we writhed in pain, but we gave birth to wind. We have not brought salvation to the earth; we have not given birth to people of the world.

The Bride is content to be engaged to Jesus. She talks about Him, tells great stories about Him, but fails to enter beyond the veil, into the Holy of Holies, where she will submit to the wooing of His heart for the nations. He longs to have a Bride for Himself who will bear fruit after His own kind. We are to be "pregnant" with the gospel of Christ!

## REPLICATING THE RELATIONSHIP

Once the gospel has produced life, that life must be nurtured. We teach others how to experience relationship with Christ by modeling it before them. In the physical, there are no schools for marriage and parenting except the homes where we live. In the spiritual, we who understand and experience Christ and His ways are to model them continually for others. As Paul demonstrated, "Whatever you have learned or received or heard from me, or seen in me—put it into practice. And the God of peace will be with you" (Phil. 4:9). We must become the present day Pauls who will model genuine, intimate intercession and travail. Then we, too, can say with Paul, "Those things you have learned, received, heard, or seen in me, do."

As mentors and teachers, we impart to others those things formed in us. Christ now asks the Bride, "You who dwell in the gardens with friends in attendance, let me hear your voice!" (Song of Songs 8:13). Our instruction is to teach others this love relationship with our heavenly Groom. We are the message. Jesus is saying to His Bride, "Let me hear your voice."

## THE SPIRIT AND THE BRIDE SAY, "COME!"

We must humble ourselves and admit our failure as the Church. We are somewhat familiar with fruit bearing. For the most part, however, in recent years the Church has been pregnant with its own seed. It has born fruit after its own kind (see Gen. 1:11,12). We have given birth to "wind." We are unable to distinguish between the work of the flesh and the work of the Spirit. We read how the cloud of smoke filled the temple in the Old Testament. However, today we cannot discern between dust and smoke: the "dust" of human activity and the "smoke" of divine activity!

Clearly, we have not brought salvation to the earth. We have not given birth to overcoming prayers for people of the world. The time has come for the Bride to understand her calling and submit to her Husband:

> Let us be glad and rejoice, and give honor to him: for the marriage of the Lamb is come, and his wife hath made herself ready. And to her was granted that she should be arrayed in fine linen, clean and white: for the fine linen is the righteousness of saints (Rev. 19:7,8, KJV).

For too long the Church has loved Him in words, but not in deeds. We have refused intimacy beyond the veil. Our heavenly Groom has prepared white linen robes for us to wear. He is knocking at the door, but we have not made ourselves ready. Even though we have been given the robes, we have refused to put them on. Like the five foolish virgins in Matthew 25:1-13, most of us have not filled our oil lamps in preparation for the wedding banquet. Time is running out.

For years the Church has looked at the Great Commission as a human evangelistic responsibility. Finally, some are beginning to see that it is to be the result of a marriage partnership. The final fruit of our relationship with Christ is the completion of the Great Commission. It is a joint effort, a united partnership between the Lord and His Bride. It is born in passionate prayer and intercession! To a lost and dying world of 2.5 billion people, the final words of Jesus are, "The Spirit and the Bride say, 'Come!'" (Rev. 22:17).

## UNVEILING THE TRUTH ABOUT YOU

1. Why does it please the Lord to call you His "Bride"?
2. Is it possible to be married to someone you hardly know? Are you living like you are married to Christ? In what areas have you distanced yourself from your heavenly Bridegroom?
3. What are some of the ways in which your relationship to Christ has been tested?
4. Have you been giving birth to wind through your busyness, career, activities or even ministry? What has this done to your relationship with Jesus?

# Come Beyond the Veil

## GOD'S CALL TO INTIMATE INTERCESSION

How lovely is your dwelling place, O Lord Almighty!
My soul yearns, even faints, for the courts of the Lord;
my heart and my flesh cry out for the living God
(Ps. 84:1,2).

Two thousand years ago Jesus hung on the cross and cried out, "It is finished!" At the sound of those words, the flesh over His heart ripped in two, redeeming fallen humanity from eternal separation with God. Heaven's windows opened and the hand of God reached into the temple tearing the veil in the Holy of Holies from top to bottom. God's heart was forever exposed to all who would seek Him. His heart was open to all who would commune with Him. His throne room was now accessible to all who would enter.

"It is finished!" Finished forever are the days when God is unapproachable; finished forever are the days when His children must stand outside as the high priest intercedes for them. God Himself initiated the level of intimate intercession that can occur only beyond the veil. Such communion with God is prayer at its deepest level. And it is available to all who will come into the "the inner chamber" of the Holy of Holies.

## THE INNER CHAMBER

Many in the Church still have questions about the inner chamber: what is this inner chamber, who should enter and how do they reach it? They erroneously believe that only intercessors are welcome. But the truth is that all believers are welcome and not all intercessors ever reach this level of communion with the Lord. There are few writings about this deeper level of intimacy in prayer, and for that reason we must learn.

First, however, let us quickly review what we have already discussed. As we discovered in chapter 5, the body, soul and spirit of a person serve as an illustration of the Old Testament tabernacle or temple. The body represents the Outer Court; the soul, the Holy Place; and the spirit, the Holy of Holies. According to the apostle Paul, we are the temple of God (see 1 Cor. 6:19). For us to attain an "inner chamber" or "Holy of Holies" intimacy with God in prayer, we must bring both the body (senses or Outer Court) and the soul (mind, will and emotions or Holy Place) under the dominion of our spirit (Holy of Holies). It is our spirit that has become one Spirit with God.

## WHAT IS THE PROBLEM?

The problem is getting your body to submit to your soul and getting your soul to submit to your spirit so that all that you are is submitted to His Holy Spirit within you. But how do you submit the outer self to the Spirit within? This is the dilemma. The more you strive to submit your body and soul to the Spirit (through concentration and focusing on the Lord), the more outwardly driven rather than inwardly drawn you become.

While struggling to submit your mind to the Lord, you anticipate the fight and become more self-conscious. Consequently, the process itself defeats you. For this reason, many have given up and walked away from an encounter that might have forever transformed them. Let me enourage you to try again.

**A Time and a Place**
First, it is vital that you pick the right time and place to help

silence your mind. Finding a place where you can spend an extended time (perhaps hours) without interruption is essential. You must not be interrupted by the phone, the door or any other distraction. If you do not schedule this time, you will never do it! Therefore, you must let the Lord be the priority of your day.

Remember, communion with the Lord is relational. As the Lover of your soul, He longs to fellowship with you. The quest for intimacy begins as you quiet your spirit and focus your mind on the Lord.

### A Posture, a Position, a Pen and a Pad

Posture is important and purely personal. You may concentrate best by sitting, kneeling or even lying face down. What is most important is the posture of your heart. If your eyes are closed, fewer distractions can lure you toward the world's pull. Remember, Jesus said that "the kingdom of God is within you" (Luke 17:21).

The natural tendency for your mind to wander is part of your "fallenness." The mind is not "reborn" as is your spirit, so it must be "renewed" moment by moment—brought under control, as the apostle Paul wrote, "into captivity." Plagued by mental aerobics, you may find yourself remembering people to call, things to do and places to go.

Early in learning this process of prayer, I fought these urges. Again, fighting these disruptions defeated my intentions to find intimacy. Such interruptions caused feelings of guilt and failure that became additional hindrances. I found myself caught in a vicious cycle, trapped in the Outer Court. Having a pen and pad close by now allows me to stop and write these thoughts down. It frees my mind from the worry of forgetting. As an honest seeker, do not let the enemy condemn you. In time, you will learn to lavish your attention, as well as your affection, freely upon the Lord.

## APPROACHING THE THRONE

After the protocol of waiting in silence before the Lord, with a heart of enthusiasm, begin to glorify...

## THE FATHER

Praise Him for His attributes. Speak to Him with abandoned affection!

> Father, I exalt Your name above every name. You are clothed with majesty and glory. I rejoice, for You are Lord. Receive all honor and respect today. I testify of Your magnificent love and testify before angels and demons that there is no other God but You. You are the only God. You are the everlasting God. You are the great I AM, the everpresent, eternal God. You are a loving Father. You are my Father. I love You, I love You.

Allow expressions of love to bubble up from within your heart. Pour out our affection upon Him. You might bless the Father for having such great love that He would sacrifice His Son Jesus for your sin. Thank Him for always being there for you, for being such a wonderful Father. You might thank Him for giving the Holy Spirit to help you walk in holiness. Do not hurry! Linger. Exalt Him with your praise! Enjoy your fellowship together.

Once immersed in worship, concentrate on...

## THE SON

Let your words become lavish with exaltation! Thank the Lord Jesus for the miracles He performed or the way He handled different situations when He was on earth.

> Jesus, You radiate with glory! As the Father escorted You into the eternal, You have gained the right to receive all honor, glory and praise! Thank You, Jesus, for the way You dealt with the woman with the issue of blood. She was so weary and discouraged after 12 long years. You treated her with such tenderness and respect when You told her, "Take heart daughter, your faith has healed you." I can almost see Your eyes of love as You looked kindly at her. In front of everyone, You blessed

and healed her. You are awesome, Jesus! Oh, I want to have that kind of compassion and love for people! You are so precious and I adore You! I delight to sit in Your presence!

Thank Him for blessings He has recently given you. Recognize the elements of His character: His mercy, His power, His patience, His disciplined life and His faithfulness. Celebrate the awesome presence of...

## THE HOLY SPIRIT

Tell Him how much you appreciate His anointing and revelation.

Praise You, Holy Spirit. You are faithful. Thank You for making known to me those things that no eye can see, no ear can hear, no man can understand. You alone have all wisdom and understanding and knowledge. I praise You Holy Spirit. Be the center of all that I pray. Rule and reign in my heart, mind and soul so that all that is spoken will bring glory and honor to the Lord.

Utter words of sincere gratitude for revealing the Word of God to you. Recollect the many whispered promises that have been fulfilled. Bless Him for helping you learn the love of God in your life. Thank Him for being your teacher. Tell Him you cherish His willingness to encourage you after miserably failing to obey His leading. Lavish your love on the Lord. Magnify Him with every ounce of breath you have.

## IGNITE YOUR WORSHIP WITH PRAISE

Remember the television commercial showing the two lovers running toward one another with arms outstretched through a beautiful green meadow? Allow your heart to reach out to Him, raising your hands as you seek His embrace. You will find He draws near to you as you ignite the spark of love with your worship and praise. "Come near to God and he will come near to you" (Jas. 4:8). He draws near to the one who brags on and appreciates Him. He is attracted to sincere praise and intimate fellowship.

The heavenly activities of worship and intercession are intertwined. In terms of a worship liturgy, this is the praise time! You are celebrating His excellency and proclaiming His faithfulness. The intimate, quiet, heart-to-heart, face-to-face encounter is yet to come. Nevertheless, this is an important part of the journey beyond the veil.

## HINDRANCES TO BREAKTHROUGH

If your attention is on your ability to sound good musically, your praise experience will be hindered. If you struggle with acceptance before the Lord, this will hinder if not prevent your breakthrough in intimacy. If your focus is centered on your own inadequacy, efforts toward intimacy will be useless. You know that a healthy relationship between two people cannot develop while either strives to perform or attain acceptance. The same is true in intimacy at this deeper level.

Your soul must not work to enter a relationship with the Lord. You should simply offer sincere affection. Spiritually speaking, the idea is the same. It is your right, as part of the Bride of Christ, to enjoy the presence and the love of Jesus. Therefore, at this stage of prayer, resist all urges to deal with your failures, flaws or sins. There will be time for that on other occasions.

Lavish affection and praise drive back the enemy. "From the lips of children and infants you have ordained praise because of your enemies, to silence the foe and the avenger" (Ps. 8:2). The enemy is left speechless. He flees at the sound of heartfelt praise for Jesus.

As your vision clears and the destination beyond the veil draws nearer, fiercely fight the inclination to love the Lord because you want something. That is both childish and selfish. You should pour adoration upon Him because you adore Him. Simply relinquish your mind, emotions and will to the living Lord. At some point in your praise, you will reach a plateau.

## THE PLATEAU

You are there when no further words can be spoken. David illustrates this, "Deep calls to deep in the roar of your waterfalls; all your waves and breakers have swept over me" (Ps. 42:7). "Deep calls to deep" means that the Spirit of God is searching all the deep things of God within your spirit, so He can reveal the deep things of God to you. No longer conscious of time and space, this holy moment ushers you into the inner sanctum. Erased from your mind are any thoughts of earthly surroundings as you are lost in your love for Him and His love for you.

It is as though you have climbed a mountain and have reached its pinnacle. With great anticipation and relief you look out across the horizon waiting for the next adventure. Standing speechless, you simply lose yourself in His presence. Instantly, all heaven celebrates your entry as a child of the King. Heaven's hosts applaud as you enter through the door of the inner chamber into the Holy of Holies. The sheer radiance of His glory envelops you.

## TRUST, THE DOORWAY TO INTIMACY

You will pass through four relational stages as you become one with your heavenly Groom. The first is the acquaintance stage. Through the new birth you become *acquainted* with God as His child. Beyond that you develop a true *friendship* with Him. Based on that friendship and your experiences with Him a deep *trust* is cultivated. This trust is the doorway then to *intimacy.*

Even now, you may find yourself uncomfortable with such abandonment to the Lord. Self-defenses are beginning to activate. Sadly, some of us have more faith in the enemy's power to deceive us than in our Savior's power to protect us. Such a conclusion implies that Satan is more relational than God. Once and for all you must settle the issue that God is passionately in love with you and will never give you a serpent for a fish, nor a stone for bread (see Matt. 7:7-11). Remember, it is God Almighty who calls us by the intimate name "My Bride." John tells us in Revelation 21:9, "Come, I will show you the bride, the wife of the Lamb."

So trust is the tear in the veil through which He leads us by the hand into His throne room or bed chamber. You can bring

........................................................................

*Trust is the tear in the veil through which He leads us by the hand into His throne room or bed chamber.*

........................................................................

your flaws, failures and concerns into His presence. Your impurities do not threaten Him. He knows your heart, and His love for you is unconditional. The loving-kindness of God will bring you to a point of cleansing and forgiveness as you submit yourself in voluntary devotion to Him.

Consistent fellowship with the Lord produces:

1. **Purity.** Time in His presence causes us to become like Him.
2. **Revelation.** Time in His presence increases spiritual sensitivity and knowledge.
3. **Discernment.** Time in His presence provides a Kingdom perception of spiritual realities.

From sacred hours of intimacy spent in His presence, you will experience "transformation by adoration." Burdens lift and frustrations dissolve as you nestle under His divine covering.

### THE EYE OF THE HURRICANE

The process of moving deeper into intimate intercession is similar to flying into the eye of a hurricane. The center of a hurricane has the lowest barometric pressure of the storm. As you experience passionate Inner Court worship, the pressures of life release you. Though the outer winds of your life may gust with strife, turmoil, confusion, pain and responsibility, as you enter the eye of the storm, you will experience a peace and calm. At the center of your spirit, where the Holy Spirit resides, there is no disturbance, only tranquility.

You have submitted your soul to God. You are changed. You have dedicated your mind to Him. Your will is now subject to His will; your emotions now intertwine with His. In complete unity, you are now cooperating with the Holy Spirit by waiting upon Him. The Lord sees that He can trust you. He becomes firmly convinced that your commitment is to His presence, not just His benefits. His response is like a tidal wave of love flowing over you. His presence is a timeless reality. The spiritual atmosphere is electric as He covers you with His royal robe. You are His and He is yours!

Absolutely speechless, the joy of total companionship is euphoric, as unsurpassed peace is yours beyond measure! It is as though you have escaped the shackles of earth and ascended into the heavenlies. Without saying a word, the Lord liberates you from care. Answers to prayer are yours without having spoken a single word. "Your Father knows the things you have need of" (Matt. 6:8, NKJV). You are experiencing the intercession of Jesus.

Another way to describe this Inner Court intercession is as if the Spirit of God were inflating your spirit like a balloon. As your soul is subject to His Spirit, the wind of God enlarges your spirit. "Again Jesus said, 'Peace be with you! As the Father has sent me, I am sending you.' And with that he breathed on them and said, 'Receive the Holy Spirit'" (John 20:21,22). As you breathe in His Spirit, your spirit is exhaled until all that fills the inner chambers is the breath of God. You move and breathe in the fullness of His life-giving presence.

Compare this to 2 Chronicles 7, when the shekinah glory came into the temple. Neither the priests nor the people could stand in the temple when the glory came. When glory comes during intimate intercession, all thoughts of time, space, hunger, personal responsibilities and needs diminish. God wraps you up in Himself. Your will is loose from self-direction, and your one desire is to relate to the Person of Christ. Your soul ceases to fight against your spirit. Instead, your soul surrenders as the Holy Spirit draws you into the Holy of Holies.

## THE HEAVENLY HOST

The Holy Spirit is the heavenly Host within the inner chambers of the Holy of Holies. He prepares and serves your spiritual food. You need only receive as you feast and fellowship at His table. You may receive a portion of revelation, or perhaps a reassuring taste of His love. He may entrust you with a prayer need. The Lord does not have to show His love by speaking words. We are spirit beings, therefore, His affection may come in gentle spoonfuls of peacefulness. You may experience intense weeping and not understand why, or groan in your spirit as "the Holy Spirit makes groaning" (Rom. 8:26). He may speak in parables, reveal symbols or give new meaning to a Scripture. Sometimes His words are simply "Dear One, I love you."

This process may happen instantly. It may take 10 minutes, or possibly 2 hours. When you are in love, time is irrelevant. Then again, you may sit silently in one another's presence. The key to unlocking the door of intimacy with Jesus is to lay down all your preconceived ideas. Leave your expectations at the door and just enjoy communion with the Lord, no matter how much or how little you experience.

## DON'T IMPOSE ON YOUR HEAVENLY LOVER

May I offer an important warning? There is no place for the self-life before the throne of God. Selfishness destroys even human relationships. This is no time for "give me's." The most frequent reason for the abortion of intimacy beyond the veil is a believer's insistence on making personal requests at inappropriate times. Sometimes, in our selfishness, we take advantage of our heavenly Lover with our impatience and greed.

We impose unfeelingly upon Him and presumptuously ask for something, even something good, when He has waited so long to have us all to Himself. The Spirit-to-spirit union breaks immediately if the offensive soul seeks to dominate.

## LORD, YOU ALONE ARE MY DESIRE

In time, the discerning Bride safe in the arms of her Bridegroom will see "that look in His eye" that communicates lovingly, *Okay beloved, what do you want from Me?* For years I took this opportunity to share my prayer requests with Him. Then one day, captivated by His grace and mercy, there seemed only one correct answer, "My Beloved Lord, I want only you." Instantly, in the unseen realm, the shouts of joy were heard in heaven as a new breakthrough occurred in the relationship between Jesus and His intercessor. I had been given the opportunity to ask for anything, instead I chose to have more of God. I rejoice in that decision daily.

Amazingly, this new victory also ushers in new authority! Unaware of the promotion in heaven's court, the believer who makes this choice waits for a response from the Lord. Imagine His delight with this choice as He answers, "Beloved, I give you more of Me." A metamorphosis occurs as the old nature falls off and the spirit is given new life beyond the veil with Him. True love has taken root.

Have you noticed that a husband and wife begin to physically resemble one another as a result of living together for years? This is true in the spiritual realm as well. Endless visitations in the prayer closet will cause you to look more like Jesus. You will be changed "from glory to glory" (see 2 Cor. 3:18). Moses, having been in His presence, returned from the mountain with such glory that he was forced to wear a veil. People will see God's glory on you too, as you spend time "on the mountain" with Him!

## INTIMACY FOR INTIMACY'S SAKE

Some say that wealthy people have difficulty distinguishing their real friends from those who befriend them simply to get something. Today's headlines are replete with stories of fortune seekers who marry for gain and leave grieving lovers in the wreakage of their greed. Surely the Lord has known His share of spiritual Brides who have sought Him simply seeking the reputation of His name and the riches of His inheritance. We, however, must approach Him with a pure and sincere desire for Him alone. Such selfless adoration blesses Him immeasurably and changes us completely.

As we enter the inner chamber, we must set aside our prayer lists and refuse to approach Him as though He were a "Santa Claus" or "Heavenly Sugar Daddy." Those lists must be set aside for another day. Now is not the time to seek revelation or a word from God. Even though He may begin to deposit nuggets of truth in our hearts, whatever is deposited must come from Him. All seeking must concern Him and Him alone. This is a time of intimacy for intimacy's sake. We are there for communion, love, devotion and to hear the burden on His heart, if He chooses to share one. This is the pinnacle of prayer! Time in the inner chamber is both the deepest and the highest moment with God that we can experience on an earthly plane.

## LORD, WHAT IS ON YOUR HEART TODAY?

The goal of time set aside in the inner chamber is to have one heart with Jesus. When you ask, "Lord, what is on Your heart today?" He may either flood you with immense revelation or He may be silent. I have experienced both. He may, as He once did with me, utter one word, "Peru."

I asked, "Lord, what about Peru?" Immediately my heart was broken. I wept uncontrollably, not understanding why. Suddenly I knew that He had spiritually enlarged me with groaning from the Spirit to bear a burden impossible for a mere mortal. It was the burden of the Almighty.

Mental images of children began to flash before my mind. That was it! I was weeping for the children in Peru. (At this point it is critical to find and follow the path of the Spirit. This becomes easy if you are sensitive to the inner stirring of the Spirit.) In this situation, as I prayed for the children of Peru, my weeping intensified. It was the Lord's way of showing me this was His burden. If I changed direction by praying for other things, the emotional upheaval would have stopped; my tears would have ceased; and the burden would have drifted away. I would have aborted the intercessory assignment for my own comfort and convenience.

Another indication that His burden is being aborted is when a "deadness" settles in your spirit. Do not be alarmed, just return to the burden the Lord first revealed to you. He may continue with the same direction for some time. On the other hand, He may move quickly through several issues. Because intercession is about His burden, we must submit willingly wherever the wind of His Spirit blows.

As I prayed for Peru, I knew when the travail stopped and the spiritual release came that my present prayer assignment for the children of Peru was completed. In some situations the Lord may give specific names, places, dates and other pertinent information. He may give Scripture to read or proclaim aloud, or you may even pray the Scripture.

Exercise discipline and do not quit praying before the breakthroughs of God are completed. If possible, the enemy and your flesh will distract you with Outer Court issues. Satan and his minions will do anything to cause you to abort God's purpose. They are absolutely terrified of what you are doing and would give anything to have the power that is available to you in prayer! Even those who pray to Satan are limited to his lesser power. Your prayer is an appeal to your Unlimited God! So fortify yourself to pray until you release the burden and have a witness in your heart of victory!

### BEARING BURDENS WITH THE HEAVENLY BRIDEGROOM

As the Bride of Christ, you will never go through any moment of life alone again. He longs to share as much with you as you are willing to receive. Not only do you have the joy of sharing in the Bridegroom's victories, but you can also share His burdens. Suppose you get a mental picture of a family member. Resist the temptation to make premature judgments or make requests of God concerning this loved one from *your* human perspective. Instead, ask, "Lord, what about this loved one?"

The Lord may tell you about a timely need. If so, in faith agree with Him concerning this burden. He may also expose the enemy's plans for harm to your loved one. For example, He may reveal to you that the enemy has designed an airplane disaster for one in your family. So with ambassadorial authority, enter warfare intercession. Fight FOR God against the devil. Pray

........................................................................

*A mature intercessor will be willing to bear the burden while God alone bears the knowledge. This is faith pressed to the limits!*

........................................................................

AGAINST the enemy's plan and FOR God's plan. If you do not know how to pray, simply agree with God. Pray, "Lord, preserve Your purpose for my loved one's life."

A more difficult intercessory assignment is when God places a burden on us without an attached assignment. In other words, you receive the burden from the Lord's heart, but you have no idea what it concerns. In this case He is asking you to bear His burden by faith, and to intercede without knowledge (Rom. 8:26). This is another opportunity for the enemy to deceive the intercessor into aborting the process. You may wrongly assume it makes no sense to bear a burden for something about which you have no knowledge. A mature intercessor will be willing to bear the burden while God alone bears the knowledge. This is faith pressed to the limits!

As the time of closure approaches, you will find yourself waiting for further instruction. When nothing else comes to your heart or mind, you might ask, "Lord, is there anything You want to say to me?" He may or may not speak to you. Guard your heart from rejection or the need to manipulate Him if He chooses not to speak. During this period, however, He may share with you the secrets of His heart. (Read Psalm 25:14.) It may be direction, revelation, affirmation or correction. The message will usually be very personal, so journal in a notebook anything He says. Ask for His interpretation and application. Keep in mind, however, He may say nothing at all. This too is His choice.

## Periods of Dryness

Never assume His silence is His absence. To do so communicates a breach of trust that says He cannot be trusted to do what is best for you. As with all relationships, silence is an indication that comfort and trust have been established.

During a prayer journey to Israel, God spoke clearly and profoundly to me. I returned home spiritually and emotionally exhausted. I also returned to a "dry time" in my prayer closet. Although soothed by the warmth of His love and sheltered in a meditative rest, all efforts of hearing His voice failed. My emotional strength was gone.

The nearness of the Lord was sweet, but there was little or no depth of the intimacy I described earlier. Through this and other experiences, I have learned that we are to faithfully come into the Inner Court with no strings attached. If we do, then periods of dryness and periods of refreshing are the same. Why? Because we have learned to enjoy the Lord simply because we love Him, not because of His gifts or the manifestations of His presence.

Intercessors should beware of the trap of trying to acquire a bigger and better "high." This is Outer Court striving. Avoid striving at all costs! Experienced intercessors submit themselves to the discipline of the dry times. Consider the seasons when the Lord is quiet in your life to be "spiritual tune-ups." During these times of transition, when He chooses not to speak, your spiritual ears are being fine tuned and opened to hearing His voice. In time, your spirit will learn to hear Him, even when He whispers.

The Lord monitors your faithfulness to Inner Court intimacy. These dry times provide the kindling that sparks a fresh gratitude, and later explodes in a blaze of passion that will thrust you into the Inner Court when He speaks to you once again!

## His Presence Awaits You
## Beyond the Veil

No words in the English language can describe the splendor that awaits us in the inner chamber. As I have journeyed with Jesus throughout the years, I have discovered that only those who continue to press into the very heart of God will find their abiding place in Him. Every believer who longs for, and lingers, and continues to want a relationship of deep communion with the Lord will have one. Friend, you can have as much of God as you want. Are you willing to invest your time and your tears? Will you let anything stop you from this deeper intimacy? Do you long to know the joy of abiding in Him?

He is waiting to commune with you (see Rev. 3:20). If you are hungry and thirsty enough, you will experience the fulfillment of Jesus' promise to all who seek, "Whoever believes in me, as the Scripture has said, streams of living water will flow from within him" (John 7:38).

I have no doubt that all earthly thrills will diminish once you taste the delicacies of this sweet relationship beyond the veil.

### UNVEILING THE TRUTH ABOUT YOU

1. In what ways have you been a selfish Bride? Have you ever felt like you were in this marriage just for what you could get? If so, are you willing to change?
2. Do you have a private place and time set aside to be alone with Jesus?
3. Have you said no to His call to enter the inner chamber? Have you become complacent in your love for Him? Are you willing to be more sensitive to Him now?
4. When struggling in prayer, do you quit? Have you been experiencing "dry periods" in your marriage to Him? Can you now understand the reason for those times?
5. Will you renew your wedding vows to Him? Will you say, "I will" when He calls you into the inner chamber? Will you abide with Him beyond the veil?

# Discussion Leader's Guide

~~~

This book has a dual purpose: (1) to rekindle the love of Jesus' Bride in order that He might find her without spot or blemish and (2) that she might partner with Him in what appears to be the last great revival before His return.

As a group leader and facilitator for the Holy Spirit, you are called to help others hear His voice rather than imposing your own personal beliefs upon those who may have different gifts or worship styles from your own.

The optimum-sized discussion group is 10 to 15 people. A smaller group can make continuity a problem when too few members attend. A larger group will require strong leadership skills to create a sense of intimacy and participation for each person.

If you are leading a group that already meets regularly, such as a Sunday School class or weekly home group, decide how many weeks to spend on the series. Be sure to plan for any holidays that may occur during your schedule.

Be creative. Although the book is only nine chapters and could be covered in as few as 6 weeks by pairing some of the chapters, it can also be fit into a 13-week quarter by spending more time on the issues of character building in chapter 6, or even the practical application of prayer as you pursue corporate intercession. Sensitivity to the members of your group and instruction from the Holy Spirit will help you to determine the course you as a leader should take.

The first session is a great time to determine the spiritual climate of your group. The following questions can be used to create a sense of unity and determine the direction you should take as a group:

1. Do you believe prayer is vital to your Christian life? Why?
2. In what ways are you hoping to see your prayer life change as a result of this class?
3. Do you believe that the Holy Spirit speaks differently to each of us and that the way we pray can be related to our spiritual gifts?
4. Have you ever had a burden to pray for someone that caused you to feel any kind of physical pressure? If so, how did you respond to it?
5. Do you have a desire to develop a more intimate relationship with Jesus?

Such questions will create a sense of identity among the class members and help them to discover their similarities.

Many individual questions may arise that will significantly contribute to the group's understanding of the subject. Group members should be encouraged to maintain lists of their questions. Suggest that they be submitted anonymously and combine them to eliminate repetition. Many questions may be answered by the time the series reaches its conclusion. It is, therefore, a good idea to wait until your last session to discuss them.

Enlist a coleader to assist with calling class members to remind them of meeting dates, times and places. Your coleader can also make arrangements for refreshments and child care.

People will have a greater appreciation for their books if they are responsible for paying for them. They will also be more apt to finish the course if they have invested in their own materials.

Be sure to have several extra Bibles available. *The Living Bible* is often helpful for people who have little or no Bible background, however, it is important to explain that the *NIV* differs considerably and will be the main version used in this book.

Be aware of the basic principles for group dynamics, such as:

1. Arrange seating in a semicircle with the leader included rather than standing in front. This setting invites participation.
2. Create a discussion-friendly atmosphere. The following tips are helpful for guiding discussions:

   a. Receive statements from group members without judgmentalism, even if you disagree with them. If they are clearly unbiblical or unfair, you can ask questions that clarify the issue; but outright rejection of comments will stifle open participation.
   b. If a question or comment deviates from the subject, either suggest that it be dealt with at another time or ask the group if they want to pursue the new issue now.
   c. If one person monopolizes the discussion, direct a few questions specifically to someone else. Or, tactfully interrupt the dominator by saying, "Excuse me, that's a good thought, and I wonder what the rest of us think about that." Talk with the person privately and enlist that person's help in drawing others into the discussion.
   d. Make it easy and comfortable for everyone to share or ask questions, but don't insist that anyone do so. Reluctant participants can warm to the idea of sharing by being asked to read a passage from the book. Pair a shy person with someone else for a discussion apart from the main group, and ask reluctant participants to write down a comment to be shared with the larger group.
   e. If someone asks you a question and you don't know the answer, admit it and move on. If the question calls for insight from personal experience, invite others to comment on it, however, be careful that this sharing is limited. If it requires special knowledge, offer to look for an answer in the library or from a theologian or minister, and report your findings later.

3. Guard against rescuing. The purpose of this group is to

learn to pray for others, not fix them. This doesn't mean that poignant moments won't come up or unhappy problems won't be shared, but the group is for sharing and prayer—not fixing others. The leader should be open and honest about wanting to grow with the group instead of coming across as an authority about the subject.

4. Start and stop on time, according to the schedule agreed upon before the series begins. This is especially important for those who have to hire a baby-sitter or arise early for work the next morning.

5. During each session, lead group members in discussing the questions and exercises at the end of each chapter. If you have more than 8 or 10 class members, consider dividing into small groups, then invite each group to share one or two insights with the larger group.

6. Be sensitive. Some people may feel comfortable praying for others, but don't force those who don't. It is necessary to set aside a time either at the beginning or end of the meeting to pray for those in need.

7. Encourage members of the group to pray daily for each other. This will perpetuate a sense of unity and love.

8. As a leader, pray regularly for the sessions and the participants, asking the Holy Spirit to cover each person throughout the week. The Lord will honor your willingness to guide His people toward a more intimate relationship with Him.

# Suggested Reading

Alves, Elizabeth. *Becoming a Prayer Warrior*. Ventura, Calif.: Renew Books, 1998.

Anderson, Neil T., and Charles Mylander. *Setting Your Church Free*. Ventura, Calif.: Regal Books, 1994.

Bickle, Mike. *Passion for Jesus*. Orlando, Fla.: Creation House, 1993.

Billheimer, Paul E. *Destined for the Throne*. Ft. Washington, Pa.: Christian Literature Crusade, 1975.

Clinton, J. Robert. *The Making of a Leader*. Colorado Springs, Co.: NavPress, 1988.

Damazio, Frank. *The Making of a Leader*. Portland, Ore.: Trilogy Productions, 1988.

Dawson, John. *Healing America's Wounds*. Ventura, Calif.: Regal Books, 1994.

——*Taking Our Cities for God*. Lake Mary, Fla.: Creation House, 1990.

Dawson, Joy. *Intimate Friendship with God*. Grand Rapids, Mich.: Chosen Books, 1986.

Deere, Jack. *Surprised by the Power of the Spirit*. Grand Rapids, Mich.: Zondervan Publishing House, 1993.

Eastman, Dick. *The Jericho Hour*. Altamonte Springs, Fla.: Creation House, 1994.

——*Love on Its Knees*. Grand Rapids, Mich.: Fleming H. Revell Co., 1989.

——*Beyond Imagination*. Grand Rapids, Mich.: Chosen Books, 1997.

Edwards, Gene. *A Tale of Three Kings*. Wheaton, Ill.: Tyndale House Publishers, 1992.

Facius, Johannes. *Intercession*. Cambridge, Kent, England: Sovereign World Limited, 1993.

Frangipane, Francis. *The House of the Lord*. Lake Mary, Fla.: Creation House, 1991.

Grubb, Norman. *Rees Howells, Intercessor.* Fort Washington, Pa.: Christian Literature Crusade, 1962.

Guyon, Jeanne. *Experiencing the Depths of Jesus Christ.* Gardiner, Me.: Christian Books, 1981.

Haggard, Ted. *Primary Purpose.* Lake Mary, Fla.: Creation House, 1995.

——*Loving Your City into the Kingdom.* Ventura, Calif.: Regal Books, 1997.

Hamon, Bill. *Prophets and Personal Prophecy.* Shippensburg, Pa.: Destiny Image Publishers, 1987.

Hansen, Jane. *Inside a Woman.* Lynwood, Wash.: Aglow Publications, 1992.

Hawthorne, Steve, and Graham Kendrick. *Prayerwalking.* Orlando, Fla.: Creation House, 1993.

Hinn, Benny. *Welcome, Holy Spirit.* Milton Keynes, England: Word Publishing, 1995.

Jacobs, Cindy. *Possessing the Gates of the Enemy.* Grand Rapids, Mich.: Chosen Books, 1991.

——*The Voice of God.* Ventura, Calif.: Regal Books, 1995.

Kinnamen, Gary. *Overcoming the Dominion of Darkness.* Grand Rapids, Mich.: Chosen Books, 1990.

Law, Terry. *The Power of Praise and Worship.* Tulsa, Okla.: Victory House Publishers, 1985.

Marshall, Catherine. *Something More.* New York, N.Y.: Avon Books, 1976.

Mills, Dick. *He Spoke and I Was Strengthened.* San Jacinto, Calif.: Dick Mills Ministries, 1991.

Mira, Greg. *Victor or Victim.* Grandview, Mo.: Grace! Publishing Co., 1992.

Murray, Andrew. *The Ministry of Intercession.* Springdale, Pa.: Whitaker House, 1982.

Nee, Watchman. *Spiritual Authority.* Richmond, Va.: Christian Fellowship Publisher, 1972.

——*The Release of the Spirit.* Cloverdale, Ind.: Sure Foundation Publishers, 1965.

Otis Jr., George. *The Last of the Giants.* Grand Rapids, Mich.: Chosen Books, 1991.

Penn-Lewis, Jessie. *Life out of Death.* Parkstone, England.

Peretti, Frank E. *This Present Darkness.* Westchester, Ill.: Crossway Books, 1986.

———*Piercing the Darkness*. Westchester, Ill.: Crossway Books, 1987.

Prince, Derek. *Shaping History Through Prayer and Fasting*. Ft. Lauderdale, Fla.: Derek Prince Ministries, 1973.

Sandford, John, and Paula Sandford. *The Elijah Task*. Tulsa, Okla.: Victory House, Inc., 1977.

Shankle, Randy. *The Merismos*. Marshall, Tex.: Christian Publishing Services, Inc., 1987.

Sheets, Dutch. *Intercessory Prayer*. Ventura, Calif.: Regal Books, 1996.

Sherrer, Quin, and Ruthanne Garlock. *A Woman's Guide to Breaking Bondages*. Ann Arbor, Mich.: Servant Publications, 1994.

———*The Spiritual Warrior's Prayer Guide*. Ann Arbor, Mich.: Servant Publications, 1992.

Silvoso, Ed. *That None Should Perish*. Ventura, Calif.: Regal Books, 1994.

Sjoberg, Kjell. *Winning the Prayer War*. Chichester, England: New Wine Press, 1991.

Smith, Rolland C. *The Watchmen Ministry*. St. Louis, Mo.: Mission Omega Publishing, 1993.

Tozer, A.W. *The Knowledge of the Holy*. San Francisco, Calif.: Harper & Row Publishers, 1961.

Wagner, C. Peter. *Breaking Strongholds in Your City*. Ventura, Calif.: Regal Books, 1993.

———*Churches That Pray*. Ventura, Calif.: Regal Books, 1993.

———*Confronting the Powers*. Ventura, Calif.: Regal Books, 1996.

———*Engaging the Enemy*. Ventura, Calif.: Regal Books, 1991.

———*Lighting the World*. Ventura, Calif.: Regal Books, 1995.

———*Prayer Shield*. Ventura, Calif.: Regal Books, 1992.

———*Praying with Power*. Ventura, Calif.: Regal Books, 1997.

———*Warfare Prayer*. Ventura, Calif.: Regal Books, 1992.

———*Your Spiritual Gifts Can Help Your Church Grow*. Ventura, Calif.: Regal Books, 1979; revised edition, 1994.

White, Tom. *Breaking Strongholds*. Ann Arbor, Mich.: Servant Publications, 1993.

# Subject Index

# Ministry Contact Information

## CONFERENCES, SEMINARS AND RETREATS

Alice and Eddie Smith, in association with the U.S. PRAYER CENTER, travel worldwide teaching on various themes related to revival and spiritual awakening. Their topics include: prayer, intercession, deliverance, worship, spiritual warfare and mapping.

If you would like information about hosting a conference with either or both of the Smiths in your church or city you can contact them toll-free at 1-800-569-4825 or complete the online invitation form located at: www.usprayercenter.org.

## PRAYERNET E-MAIL NEWSLETTER

Alice Smith is senior editor of this biweekly, innovative, up-to-the-minute e-zine for praying Christians and church leaders. It's *free*! Join thousands worldwide who receive PrayerNet. Send a blank e-mail to <prayernet-subscribe@usprayercenter.org> or sign up online at www.usprayercenter.org.

Alice and Eddie Smith publish the monthly postal newsletter, *UpLink*. For your *free* subscription to *UpLink*, mail your name and postal address (U.S. Only) to U.S. PRAYER CENTER, 7710-T Cherry Park Dr., Suite 224, Houston, TX 77095, or fax it to 713-466-5633.

## OTHER BOOKS BY ALICE AND EDDIE SMITH

- *Intercessors: How to Understand and Unleash Them for God's Glory* (ISBN: 0-9653768-3-4)

- *Intercessors and Pastors: The Emerging Partnership of Watchmen and Gatekeepers* (ISBN: 0-9653768-2-6)

- *The Advocates: How to Plead the Case of Others in Prayer* (ISBN: 088419-756-5)

- *Drawing Closer to God's Heart: A Totally Practical, Non-Religious Guide to Prayer* (ISBN: 0-88419-778-6)

You will find a complete catalog of their books and materials and may purchase online at www.usprayercenter.org or www.prayerbookstore.com or call 1-800-569-4825 or 713-466-4009.

## THE *BEYOND THE VEIL* STUDY GUIDE

Many churches, small groups and prayer cells use *Beyond the Veil* as a study course. We have developed the *Beyond the Veil Study Guide* as an accompaniment to this increasingly popular book. It is excellent for individual or group study. Order online at www.prayerbookstore.com. For quantity price discounts or to order by phone call 1-800-569-4825.

## CONTACT INFORMATION

U.S. PRAYER CENTER

7710-T Cherry Park Dr., Suite 224

Houston, TX 77095

Ph: 713-466-4009

Fx: 713-466-5633

Toll-free: 1-800-569-4825

Email: usprayercenter@cs.com

Websites: www.usprayercenter.org and

www.prayerbookstore.com